CRUISING AND BRUISING
IN CYBERSPACE:

A GUIDE TO ONLINE DATING
AFTER FORTY

ISBN-10: 1-4196-6878-1
EAN13: 978-1-4196-6878-4

Interior formatting/cover design by
Rend Graphics 2007
www.rendgraphics.com

Published by:
BookSurge Publishing, LLC.
www.booksurge.com

To order additional copies, please visit:
www.amazon.com
or
www.onlineinternetdatingguide.com

ACKNOWLEDGMENTS

I wish to thank my cousin Andi and my friend Erna who introduced me to the concept of online dating and also those men and women who shared their experiences with me. A special place in my heart exists for my daughter, Jeniffer Menks; stepdaughter, Michelle Ludwig; and dear friends who laughed and listened patiently to my stories and encouraged me to write this book. Linda Bernal, Linda Florey, Kelly Mcintosh, and Carol Reed soothed my bruises, shared my joys, gave wonderful advice, and provided support systems and great conversations. These dear persons also helped to untangle and rectify my convoluted sentences, dangling modifiers, and other grammar naughties. However, any remaining illiteracies are the result of English being my first language.

DEDICATION

This book is dedicated to those persons who have helped me along the path to learning more about them and consequently learning more about myself and my journey towards fulfillment, contentment, love, and compassion.

TABLE OF CONTENTS

INTRODUCTION

After seventeen years of marriage my husband died and suddenly I became a widow. Eventually, after sorting out my life, I felt that I was ready to find someone special again with whom to share my life. I wanted a best friend, partner, playmate, and lover for the rest of my journey. I dated a lot before our marriage, but times were different then and now I was way out of practice. Twenty-five years ago my girlfriend and I explored various ways to meet men. We went to Laundromats even though we had our own washers and dryers, joined various groups, and took classes where by chance we hoped to meet the man of our dreams. We went to bars where we met men who posed as single but were really married, alcoholics, players, and so forth. I eventually met my husband at the athletic club where I played racquetball and did aerobics. We had been members there for four years, but our paths never crossed until a chance encounter.

Now single again, the question was where to meet men who had something in common with me and would be potential partners. Earlier when I was still married, I met with my cousin Andi in Las Vegas who was there to meet someone that she had met online. She shared some of her experiences with me and found online dating to be a good way for her to meet interesting men. A couple of years later when I became a widow, my friend Erna talked about her adventures with online dating. This idea was a new one for me and seemed to be an excellent way to meet men that I normally would never encounter in my daily life. I was a busy professional woman and had little time and desire to lurk around town to meet men. So I began my occupation of cruising and bruising in cyberspace. Boy did I learn a lot! This required a whole set of special skills and cyberspace smarts. I shared my stories about online dating with others and they shared theirs with me. We all laughed, smiled, cried, and were amazed at the things we experienced in online dating. It is truly an adventure. You will meet a wide variety of people and learn a lot, not only about them, but yourself. You will learn more about what you want and need and do not want and need. You will learn more about your excess baggage and new vistas will open for you. Your friends will be anxious to call you to find out about your latest adventures. In any event, you will have very entertaining stories to share with others and perhaps even write a book about it.

I decided to write this book to share the collective wisdom and experiences that I gained as a result of my cruising and bruising in cyberspace along with those of the numerous persons I interviewed and conversed with regarding their experiences. My purpose is to provide a guide for persons who are considering or participating in online dating in order to maximize their positive results. Most of the persons I talked with were over forty years of age.

I have intentionally not identified any one in particular; however, the character and actions of some of the people we met may render them recognizable which is unavoidable even though no other identifying information is given.

My best wishes to each of you who are looking to meet someone special and are contemplating or are engaged in online dating. This guide is meant to give you additional cyberspace smarts, increase the effectiveness of your cruising, and decrease the amount of bruising in the adventure of online dating. Successful strategies, experiences, stories, and mistakes are presented so that you can learn from them. This book was written to help you to figure out how to find and attract compatible persons and not give up because you lack the skills to utilize online dating to its fullest benefits. I encourage you to develop your *cybersmarts* and *cyberflirting* skills to a higher level and try online dating with the information that you have gathered from this book to help you to find well-matched prospects to date.

I have organized this book into sections that take you through the entire process of online dating starting with *Why Online Dating?* The following section begins with details concerning very basic information about computers, the Internet, and online searches and online dating sites. Next are guidelines for the art of writing an engaging profile, headline, and name; posting photographs, and searching for and contacting potential matches (cyberflirting). The third and forth sections, *Safety Cybermarts* and *Checking Them Out*, gives specific advice to help you protect yourself in online dating and checking people out. Next is the section on *No, thanks* which describes ways to constructively and kindly say that you are not interested in someone who contacts you. Of course you will meet people who sound interesting to you and the following section, *Yes*, discusses issues such as how soon do I answer? When and how do I continue offsite? The remaining sections of the book present highly informative information and anecdotal stories about some reported scenarios and advice that will further develop your cybersmarts such as when he or she *Vanishes into Thin Air, Home Runs, Common Mistakes*, and *Set Your Radar for These*. I end the book with the section called *Number 47*, which inevitably includes Cinderella and Prince Charming finding each other, along with many other reported positive outcomes of online dating.

Why Online Dating?

I've dated a lot during the past year and almost all of these dates were with persons that I met online. In fact, I only met one-person offline to date. Although I haven't met Mr. Right, yet, I have had a lot of fun, some great relationships, a healthy sex life, and learned that I am desirable. Not so bad, huh?

The Internet has greatly changed how we communicate, giving us opportunities to search for information about almost anything and greatly increasing our exposure to vast resources. The main advantages to using the Internet for online dating are: 1) it gives you a way to view, screen and meet an extraordinary amount of available men and women who are also looking for someone, 2) it helps you screen for persons who match you and gather information about them before making an initial contact, 3) it is quick and efficient, 4) you can do it from anywhere you have an Internet connection, 5) you can remain anonymous for as long as you wish, and 6) you can exit from communication easily. These are strong reasons to engage in online dating as a means to meet people to date.

Despite these strong reasons for online dating, this can be a scary move for the pre-Internet generations who are used to more traditional ways of meeting people to date. Yes, using technology as your middleman can seem a bit cold and unfamiliar, but with the help of this book and some experience under your belt, you soon will be cruising merrily along on the cyberspace-dating highway and in the mainstream.

It's raining men (and women)

Online dating exposes you to endless numbers and varieties of men and women who are also searching for someone to date (or other such things which I will go into later in this guide, and who fortunately are the minority). Online dating is very popular and becoming increasingly commonplace. There are many fine men and women online. The numbers of persons who are or have been involved in online dating range from 25-50 million. Every week thousands more sign up and the fastest growing group is older than 40 years of age. It is not embarrassing to be on line or to tell someone that you are. You are in good company (most of the time). The Internet serves to introduce you to hundreds and hundreds of people depending on your endurance for cruising.

Online dating is not a last resort! You will be able to select from a wide variety of men and women whom you most likely would never otherwise meet. When was the last time you were exposed to so many available singles? Why limit yourself to only those persons you might meet through chance in your daily life? Remember that my husband and I belonged to the same racquet club for four years before we met by chance. Following are only a few of reported experiences with online dating:

I am very career oriented and work long hours. The last thing that I want to do at the end of a long day is go to a bar on the chance that I might meet a charming lady. I have found online dating a real boon to my social life. Within the click of a mouse I can screen hundreds of women and find potential compatible persons.

Mary and I were introduced to each other on an Internet dating site. After corresponding anonymously through the site, we began talking on the phone. We met a few weeks later and the chemistry was there. I feel that I have found that needle in the haystack, my soul mate. We were married two years ago and are expecting our first child next month.

After my divorce, I felt that I would never have a relationship again. How would I meet people and learn to date again? I did not feel that I was a sexy being and attractive. My kids kept after me to sign up on an online dating site. Since then, I have had my dating ups and downs, but am learning to do it and once again and I feel frisky and desirable.

What a hoot! So many men, so little time!

I love to hike, raft, and climb mountains and have finally found a special someone who shares my passion for these activities. Although I have joined groups with persons of similar leanings, I never met that special someone until I searched on the Internet.

I haven't had a date in over a year. I guess it's time I took some action and try online dating.

My son met his fiancé online.

Narrowing the field

Online dating allows you to cast a wide net and preview many prospective dating partners. Some sites provide you with personality tests or profiles to complete and then send you potential matches. Most allow you to customize your search in terms of age, interests, geographical location, nationality, race, children, and height. You can go to specialized sites to meet people such as those with certain religious preferences, eating preferences, sexual orientations, dog lovers, single parents with children, country or cowboy/cowgirl orientations, professionals, nationalities, and even uniformed and emergency services persons. You can narrow the field to persons with specific criteria that are very important to you.

You also can get some additional information about persons without having to ask or contact them such as whether they have ever been married, if they live alone, what pets they have, what their interests are, their vocation and so forth. Several sites have the person complete a personality test or write essays, which give additional information about them and what they are looking for. Many sites have photograph-posting options where you can actually see what the person looks like. Thus, you can gather a great deal of information before you decide whether or not to contact them. If the person does not appeal to you, then you can follow May West's quote "Next" and quickly move on to the next prospect.

Faster than a speeding bullet

Online dating is quick and easy and much less painful than hanging out somewhere hoping to meet *the one* or even anyone. No other way of seeking dates compares with the Internet's speedy ability to bring so many available single people in contact with each other and exchange information. The right one for you may be just a click away. You can also be exploring several potential matches at the same time. Initial contact is easy and no one knows about your other prospects unless you tell them. Talk about efficiency! Many people explore several potential matches, but you need to keep your information about each one straight. Strategies for developing good organizational information systems about potential matches are examined later. Internet dating is designed to enable quick and efficient initial contacts. How can you beat that?

Anytime, anywhere, and you don't need to wear clean underwear

You can surf the Internet any time of day and be at your scruffy worst. You do not need to put on make-up, clean underwear, shave, or look normal. You can also leave your lair if you have a laptop with a wireless Internet connection. If you are a Starbucks regular, you can hook up from there and sip your latte while you continue your search. More and more facilities are making wireless connections available to their patrons. If you are so fortunate as to be somewhere out of the country, you can hook up from an Internet café anywhere in the world for nominal rates and you do not even need your own computer. Back in the USA there are Kinko's, Internet cafes, or even your public library to name a few other places that have access to computers with Internet connections.

And nobody knows my name

Aha, and there you sit in some unknown locale behind a computer doing who knows what else and nobody knows your name — unless of course you tell them. You have anonymity. You might post your picture, which is definitely a good idea, and you have a screen name, which should be something catchy that you choose that is NOT, I repeat NOT, your recognizable name nor your email address. (More about choosing a screen name later.) You are entirely in control of when you release your real name to other parties, besides of course the online dating service you are using. The service most likely wants your real name, real e-mail address, and real credit card number and approval to charge their fees. Some sites are free, but note that these usually offer less features and less privacy.

Escape routes

If you have maintained your anonymity, meaning you have not given out your real name, email, phone number etc. to someone, it is quite easy to break off communication. The ways to do this vary with the online dating site. Most of the fee-based sites give you the option to not respond and block communication at any time. Many enable you to block senders from communicating with you and even more severely, to delete them from viewing and contacting you. Do not fear deleting someone as they are merely blocked from your site and continue alive and well and able to annoy others or hopefully find their true love elsewhere. Ah, but the brunt of this is that you can be at the other end of this process and yourself be excommunicated, thus a bruise as you cruise, or possibly a sigh of relief on your part. **Do not take it personally even though it is you being excommunicated.**

Everyone has something in particular that he or she is looking for and just because it does not match, does not mean that there is anything wrong with you. It also does not necessarily mean that there is anything wrong with them either, although we might prefer to think so. Remember each of you is looking for specific criteria and this is not personal.

Escaping for good from the service you have selected such as Match.com; JDate.com, eHarmony.com, etc. may not be so easy for two common reasons. 1) the clause that you may have missed that renews you automatically and 2) your profile may not be removed unless you specifically request that it be removed even though you can no longer access it. Thus, when you are no longer on the service people can see you, but you cannot be heard. People may continue to email you and you will never know and they will not get a response and will nurse their rejection (unless they have learned not to personalize this because there are many reasons for excommunication).

F. Ludwig

Also the way to contact the site to quit service is not always that easy to find. Be sure that you know how to unsubscribe and do so when you wish to quit the online dating site and take your profile listing with you.

GETTING STARTED

You need to have some very basic computer knowledge such as how to turn the computer on, connect to the Internet, send and receive e-mail, and surf the Web. If you lack this knowledge and skill, you may need to consult one of the many books available on these subjects, pick a friend's brain, or see the *Help* section in your computer or manual. This knowledge will enable you to do many things in addition to online dating and will be well worth your time and open you to many new horizons for communicating and finding information about almost anything.

The right stuff

Hardware

First of all you need to have access to a computer from the 21st century. Models older than 3 years are less efficient and limit the speed and options you might have. People will label you and your computer a dinosaur if it is older. At the time of this writing, I admit to all those who care and to those who do not, that I am using a 2001 computer. If it bothers anyone so much, I will accept a nice new one with all the bells and whistles, especially with DVD so I can watch movies and save huge amounts of information such photos, video and voice clips etc. This, however, may be TMI (too much information) for me. You do not have to have state of the art equipment to engage in online dating.

You need something with your computer that will enable you to connect to the Internet. The slowest means to connect to the Internet, and considered by most to be a dinosaur, is by a modem that utilizes the telephone line. You will have lots of time to do your nails, watch the half time show, finish your laundry, eat a bowl of ice cream, play a few hands of solitaire, and catch up with your dirty dishes as you wait for your bytes of information to inch their way through cyberspace via the telephone line. If you do not have a separate telephone line for your computer, no one will be able to call you when you are on line. The phone companies have faster systems and DSL works well. However, at this time the fastest kid on the block is the cable. Thus you have the bus, train, and airplane modes of transportation. The faster it is, the more information (especially graphics) can be uploaded, sent and received before you die of boredom waiting, decide to do something else entirely, or forget what you originally started out to do.

Finding online dating sites on the Internet

There are hundreds of sites to choose from to launch your foray into online dating and I cannot tell you which are right for you. This is something that you will have to try for yourself to see which best suits what you are looking for. Although I will mention several well-known sites, I have not constructed a table of the most popular sites because information and prices are constantly changing. Instead, I have tried in this section to give you guidelines and information that will help you locate appropriate websites for you.

If you have never done an Internet search before, all you have to do once on the Internet is find the Search area. Again there are many search engines to choose among. Most common are Google (www.google.com) and *Yahoo!Search* (www.search.yahoo.com). There are even search engines that search other search engines such as *WebCrawler* and *Metacrawler*. Visit http://www.lib.berkeley.edu/TeachingLib/Guides/ if you would like to read an excellent review and explanation of search engines. Enter key words into your search engine such as online singles or dating online and you will find hundreds of options and resources. These can be accessed directly from the search engine by clicking on the link.

When you conduct your search, you will find reviews of online dating sites, listings of conventional dating sites with large numbers of singles such as Match, American Singles, and Great Expectations or religion specific ones such as JDate and Christian Singles to name a few. If you are a vegetarian, a lesbian, a firefighter, a dog lover, looking for casual sexual encounters, or of any other ilk, there is a niche resource specifically for you. You will find a wide variety of sites and advice from which to choose. No matter what you are looking for, there is more than likely a site for you.

This brings us to a very important question for you to answer. Honestly, what is it that you are really looking for? The best website for you is determined by knowing who you are and what you want. If it is casual sex with no strings, then a website such as www.Lavalife.com or www.adultfriendfinders.com may be for you. If you are looking for a committed monogamous relationship with someone of your race, sexual orientation, special interests, or religion you might choose a website specifically catering to this type of person. You may also choose a website such as www.Match.com or www.Yahoo!Personals.com that have a huge pool and wide variety of members. Match is the largest and it may offer one-stop shopping. JDate (www.jdate.com) is the first and largest site for Jewish singles and has many features, but is one of the most expensive. There are many sites for Christian singles and other religions as well. The downside to the very large websites is the number of competitors you have. Yes, you have more fish in the sea, but the sea is full of other potential contenders. You may find yourself overwhelmed with the choices or number of contacts you receive. Hmmm, I should only have such problems!

You could also choose to join more than one online dating website, but keep track of who is from where and be realistic concerning how many you can handle at one time. Remember, too, that choosing a site is not a lifetime commitment and you can change anytime you wish.

Online dating websites also vary in the features that they offer. I particularly like ones that allow me to see who viewed me, keep track of my sent and received emails, block persons I chose from contacting me, and allow at least four photographs to be posted. Other possible features include video and voice profiles, anonymous cell phone cyberflirting, chat rooms, free response to email, and hide profile on line. Some sights have compatibility inventories that help you learn more about yourself and what you are looking for. Match.com also offers advice from none other than Dr. Phil.

Some online dating sites are free and are more like personal ads. They generally offer fewer features than the ones that require paid subscriptions. Because of this, they may attract people who are less serious or willing to expend the energy or money. This is probably not the best market to shop for a long-term relationship. Check these out carefully and see if there are any protections for your privacy.

MySpace (www.myspace.com) is another free site that some, especially persons under 30, find to be a good source for connecting with and making friends and oftentimes sharing things that best not be shared in a public forum. The problems with MySpace.com are that is not specifically a dating site and it is difficult to remain anonymous and control who sees your web page. There are no filters and people can easily make up anything they wish, especially themselves. Be very very careful since several articles have appeared in newspapers across the nation concerning underage daughters being sexually abused by adults they met on this site and also that virus writers were targeting MySpace

Many subscription online dating sites allow you to view persons who meet criteria you specify. It is best to check these out to see if they have the features and kind of people that you are looking for. However, you usually cannot contact the people you see and they cannot contact you until you subscribe, which usually means parting with some money. However, this is usually cheaper than your bar bills and memberships to groups and organizations in order to meet people. I highly recommend that you preview several sites first to see if it has a good selection of the type of person that you are looking to meet. The catch is that you usually have to fill out a profile or take a personality test first to get into the site to preview. This is not a pleasant task, but the pay-off is worth it. It gets you to think about what you actually might say and what qualities you are looking for. If you are serious about finding relationships, you have to put in serious time and effort.

Some sites such as eHarmony (www.eharmony.com) give you the free results of their 29 level, 500-question compatibility test, which can be informative. True.com offers a free trial and the "True Compatibility Test", which claims to be the most comprehensive online personality and matchmaking test in the dating enterprise. Matches are based on the assessment of 99 distinct dating-relevant factors. If you have the perseverance to complete these, you most likely demonstrate much more of the stick-to-it-iveness needed to travel the cyberspace highway to find what you want. The rest will be a piece of cake. These are the dues you pay to be able to screen the service. You want to select a website that has the type of person you are looking for. The right one(s) for you may take some time to find and involve some trial and error.

Profiling

Completing a profile, personal inventory, or personal ad should be done with care and accuracy because it is the first impression you give. It is used as a basis for searching for your matches and is also how you market yourself. **Do not take this process lightly.** No one has told me that they enjoy this profiling process, in fact most find it difficult and hard work. A well-written and engaging profile is crucial to enabling you to find and attract the types of persons whom you are looking for.

Online dating sites vary in what they ask for in their profiles. The free ones tend to be less structured. Jdate.com is one of the most informative and structured sites. Match.com also provides structure and basic information that you complete. You are usually asked to write an opening about yourself, what you are looking for, your interests, likes and dislikes and basic information about age, ethnicity, income, type of job, number of children, lifestyle, and body type.

Some such as eHarmony.com have you do personality inventories that aim to help you learn more about yourself and the type of person who matches you along certain dimensions. I emphasize certain dimensions. For example, I am very fond of animals and do wildlife rehabilitation and am very opposed to trophy hunting. Yet, I was matched several times with men whose photographs had them proudly standing among dead animal heads that were mounted on their walls. We matched for love of outdoors and animals and this was the criterion used in the match. Nothing is perfect.

Just as you can have someone design your website, you can find people who will help you design a jazzy profile for a fee. Where do you find these persons? Of course you will find them by conducting an online search. Many online dating services and websites offer suggestions as well. The following section will provide you with some important points and tips to consider when you compose your profile. Certainly have a friend who knows you well read it over and give you an opinion. The opposite sex's viewpoint also is important.

What's in a name?

When you create an account and a profile on a particular site, you will be asked to create a screen name. It is advisable to choose a screen name that is NOT related to your real name or e-mail address in the interest of anonymity. It is best to select a screen name that characterizes some aspect of yourself that will attract the kind of person you are looking for and tells something about you. This also is an important part of your first impression and another opportunity to create a strong one. Coming up with a great screen name requires thought and using your given name is bland and you can do better. Sexy user names may be banned from some websites and is not what you wish to use if you are looking for a real relationship. If you are out to play only, names like

Sexycat, Blond Bombshell, or *Studmuffin* might work for you. I suggest that you use names that are descriptive and playful such as *Irish Eyes* or *Joie de Vivre.* Some people I know have named themselves after their dog which may be fine for dog wanting to meet dog, but confusing when referring to a two-legged creature.

You may find that the name you want to use is already in use. There are millions of people using online dating and finding an unused name is not that easy, no matter how creative you happen to be. In order to use a screen name that you like but is already in use, you may need to add something to it such as a number. For example, you may wish to use the name *skier* but the site tells you that another member already has that name. You may have to use *skier123* instead. If this one is already in use you could select some other random numbers such as *skier289.* A name is one of the first things the person sees and identifies your profile and your emails. This can turn people on, off, or leave them indifferent. For example, consider the following screen names and pay attention to your reaction to each one of them: *looking4u, beachbum, jollyjoe, 14978, sailaway, high maintenance, machoman, kindandgentle, ElCid, David 34879, Jersey girl, MarshaM, smartandfun, Keeper, TheOne.* Which ones intrigue you and which turn you off or leave you neutral?

Headliners

Some websites ask you to include a headline, which is the first thing along with your photo and screen name that others see about you. These give a first impression and play a significant role whether someone reads further. Think very carefully about how you present yourself. This is your sound byte, your opportunity to capture the attention of potential suitors. Don't waste it! If you are blessed with good wit, put it to good use. Be as creative as you can, think outside of the box, and avoid clichés. This should grab attention and make others want to read further about you. The headline does not have to have any real depth since your profile will provide this. The headline is your hook. You have lots of competition out there and you want to do everything you can to be noticed. Avoid generic, bland, and overused ones like:

> Looking for Mr. Right

> Caring Man Seeks Caring Woman

> Searching for My Soul Mate

Better choices might be something like:

> Wanted, best friend, playmate, and lover

> Able to leap tall buildings in a single bound

> Better than hot chocolate

Show the real shining you

The next step involves creating a profile of yourself. The first thing to consider when writing your profile is to show the real you. If you are seriously looking for a relationship and not a pen pal, one-night stand, or free dinner, it is essential that you be honest and sincere, especially about your weight and age. Be sure to post current photographs of yourself. Lying about, or shall we say misrepresenting, these may get your foot in the door with someone but you can almost be sure that will be as far as you get. People do not like to be deceived and are likely to feel set up. Many men and women described these experiences to me and were very turned off, angry, and befuddled that the person tricked them. Your date may be polite and you may have a pleasant time, but you are likely to be the only one having a good time. He or she might also be rude and not be particularly kind. Honestly present yourself if you wish to meet someone who appreciates you as you are. Believe it or not, someone will want you as you really are. If you have something that you wish to change and that can be changed such as weight, smoking, drinking, and drugs; work on these **before** you do your profile and get online. Fix it if you can first and do not lie about it. For those things you cannot change such as age and height, learn to accept these and incorporate the positive aspects into your self-image. For example, I am tall and not petite and these things about me cannot be changed; if someone likes shorter petite women, I may not be their match. So be it, there are many men who like tall women, thank goodness!

Part of showing the real you also involves including things about you that make you unique and give a picture of you as an individual. Include your best characteristics, traits, skills, and something quirky about you (not kinky, but quirky). Instead of listing adjectives and nouns, use specific examples, which are much more interesting than listing qualities and interests. For example, the following are frequently found in essays online:

> I am caring, well informed, funny, like animals, photography, and adventure travel.

This could be improved to read:

> I read the Washington Post and New Republic regularly and keep up to date with foreign affairs such as the Muslim insurrection in Thailand and sheep shearing contests in New Zealand. I volunteer socializing dogs at the local animal shelter and photographing them. Purina just bought one of my photographs and will use it on their new dog food bags. At last my talents have been recognized and I have gone to the dogs. Tanzania and the animals of the Serengeti were my latest travel focus. Next, I plan to visit the Amazon, search for Tarzan, and race a sloth.

Instead of "I enjoy getting together with friends" you might say, "I enjoy having dinner with friends, especially when they do the cooking and have great wine."

You want to strike that balance between showing your stellar qualities and being a braggart. Do not be negative nor put anyone down, especially your ex. Humor is very good and so is sincerity. Show your personality and be different, do not just say you are. Your profile should have a conversational tone to it. It may help you to start talking out loud about whom you are, your strengths, and what you are looking for. Use specific examples: What have you accomplished? What lies ahead for you? Let your essay be different from the others, just as you are different. Humor is good. Let your personality shine through.

Your target audience is the kind of people who have the qualities that you value. Your essays are extremely important and if you are serious about finding that special relationship, you need to take the time to write these as well as you can or find someone to help you out with this. These assistants can also be found by searching the Internet. You cannot control how you look, but you do have control over how you present yourself. Write a detailed profile that separates you from the hundreds of others online. If you get a poor response or responses from persons you do not want to attract, then you may need to edit and make changes in your profile. You may be presenting an aspect of yourself that is taken differently than you mean it or you might have emphasized something that is not really important to your identity. You want to stand out from the crowd and not write as the others do.

This is not a time for true confessions. I repeat **this is not a time for true confessions.** Do not pour your heart and soul out in a profile. Rather than advertising your baggage, work on it and lighten it up. In order to begin online dating, you should be in a good place emotionally. Cruising in cyberspace has some bruising to it and may not be for those who are feeling particularly vulnerable, insecure, or nursing a broken heart. You want to be confident and favorably advertise yourself. Also do not be negative about being online by writing such things as, "I cannot believe that I am doing this." or "My kids put me up to this." After all, the person who is reading your profile is also online.

Stop and think and jot down a list of your true shining characteristics and specific unique things about yourself such as a special interest, hobby, or accomplishments. For example, I rehabilitate wildlife. So I could turn this into, "I volunteer rehabilitating wildlife and find it so rewarding to be able to release a well animal back to its natural environment." Perhaps you just returned from a trip to the Amazon where you met a medicine man. Perhaps you are restoring a Victorian house to live in or you plan to visit Tibet. You might have run in a marathon, recently that is. Present the real you, not as you were years ago. A man I met online presented a very active lifestyle of riding horses, working out, running a marathon, boating, hiking and so forth. Unfortunately, he had not done much, if any, of these things for a long time. I was attracted by the man of twenty years ago and now is now. Be enthusiastic about yourself and what you have to offer. Include a fun short description of hobby. A word of caution, you will see *honest, caring, ready for the woman/man of my dreams, love to laugh* extremely often. Avoid these clichés. Say this by example instead: "I am truthful in my relationships with others and seek this from my match." Some persons use the words, "high morals" to describe themselves. Now what does this mean? Are they conservative, traditional, judgmental, right wing; do they adhere to a very strict rigid moral code or what? Examples would be better such as "I value commitment to family, monogamy, attend church/synagogue regularly and live by the Golden Rule."

Remember as your write your profile that your goal is to pique interest and get others to want to learn more about you and meet you. This is all about marketing yourself and you need a good promotion. A good promotion is one that gives reasons why your product is worthwhile. Avoid false advertising. Write a friendly and unique opening line such as: "Looking for first mate", "Looking for Mr. Right", "Nature boy seeks mate for swinging in the trees to movies to ocean to dance and share happy, loving life". Show interest in another party that invites them to respond to you. For example, "Enough about me, tell me about you."

Your profile may also serve to exclude persons with whom you have important differences. For example:

She: We matched in many ways regarding travel, adventure, but I listed my politics as middle of the road.

He: While you seem like an adventurous soul who has fun in life, I'm afraid our different political leanings would be a deal breaker. I'm far left of center. For me, shared politics are an important part of the equation.

This puts the deal breakers right up front and serves to keep each of you from wasting time when something essential for one of you does not match. If you state that you are looking for *a gorgeous woman who makes heads turn*, this may turn off the very type of woman that you might be looking for and show you up as shallow. Women may not respond because they do not think of themselves as gorgeous, and the gorgeous ones will be turned off as well. Using the word, *girl* to refer to a grown woman often indicates a weak man looking for a trophy rather a real flesh and blood woman with some substance and maturity.

Online services such as eHarmony.com have you take personality inventories that you can reveal when, if and how you are ready. Matches they send will be based on your personality inventory. However, you can search for matches based on criteria that you choose. It is equally important to be honest when you complete these inventories so that you will attract matches that are more likely to be compatible.

Ask your friends what they think are your best qualities and what they think is important to you. This can give you some insights and also help with the blocks we might have recognizing and stating our best traits and those that make us unique.

You oughta be in pictures

Most websites allow more than one photograph and the number varies among them. The importance of a good photograph cannot be overestimated because it is one of the first things that are seen in viewing your profile. It can draw people in or send their fingers to the next profile and you off into cyberspace. A picture can also give an indication of possible chemistry.

Many people will not respond to profiles that do not have photos posted for several reasons. First of all, with so many fish in the sea, why bother with faceless ones? Another reason is that people who do not post photos may be married or still in a relationship, which is the most common reason many of us have experienced when we contacted the no photo, posted person. There is a reason they oughta be in pictures-NOT! Optimist that I am, I preferred at first to think that the reason for no photo was that the person was too well known or some high profile professional who would not post. I have yet to find this to be the case; there was an additional reason the person did not seek exposure. Some people say that they do not want anyone to discover that they are on the Internet looking for dates. Well, if they see your face online, it is because they or someone close to them is online, too. Online dating is mainstream and full of highly respectable and desirable people. Millions of people are online and meeting significant others every day

Many sites ask you to post photos of yourself. If you do not have a camera, borrow a digital one and take various pictures of yourself or ask friends, kids, people on the street, and anyone else who can push a button to help you. You can buy a cheap disposable digital camera, go to a copy center and have photos scanned into a digital file on a disc or CD.

Post a recent photo; in fact post several that show different sides of you. You might include a professional photo, a few of you doing your favorite public activities, one with your pet, and a full body shot. Show yourself and make your life look interesting. Show who you are and look happy! No cheesecake, please! The site may not approve your picture and it turns off serious long-term matches. Legs are nice to show for both men and women. Even if you do not think your looks are your best attribute, still post a recent smiling and engaging picture of yourself. Choose photos that make you look approachable, enthusiastic, and friendly. This is not the place to post a *Glamour Shot*. This type of photo is usually not representative of how you actually appear and is no different from lying and misrepresenting yourself. It sets up unreal expectations that lead to disappointment and the game is up as soon as you meet the person. Disappointed dates are not usually good dates, as if you need to be told that!

Some of the photos I see online amaze me; for example, a photo of someone scowling, frowning, and looking bored or depressed. These set a negative tone. A straightforward smiling pose is best. Also, do not use photographs that have been doctored and we see a part of another person who has been taken out of the shot. Who wants to see the hand or such of their ex? Plus, we realize that he/she could do this to us if our relationship does not work out. Others have a younger person with them whom we hope are their children. Neither is this the place for family or group photos. A picture of you with your pet is OK if you are looking for a pet lover and someone who thinks your little Snookums is cute. If this is not that essential to you, leave Snookums out of your photographs.

Next you are ready to have your profile uploaded onto the service's website. Several sites have to approve your profile and photographs before these are published on the site. You can also edit your profile and add or delete photographs at any time. I suggest that you keep these up to date for the reasons stated above. You can also tweak your profile if you are not getting the types of responses that you are looking for.

Searching for your matches

Now that you have uploaded your profile and paid subscription fees you are ready to resume cruising and have access to all members of the online service to search for and contact. The key is to search effectively and find your best possible matches. If your online dating service provides a match service, you can set the parameters for potential matches. These parameters usually involve age range, height, geographical location, body type, religion and other things that are included in profiles. You list your preferences for a match and bingo you get immediate search results. Matches on some sites are sent to you on a regular basis. You can change your preferences for searches at any time and some websites allow you to save multiple criteria searches.

Start by casting a wide net to get an idea of the wide variety of fish in the sea. This will also help you to refine what it is that you are looking for. Just because you set your search criteria broad does not mean that you have to contact everyone or go out with them; however you will not have the choice at all if they do not match your criteria. Your dream partner may not exist and some of your criteria might have to be broadened. For example, you may only want to meet women between the ages of 40-45. What if a 46 year old woman met your other criteria? You would never see her because you would be omitting every person who does not exactly meet the criteria you set. So pick a wider age range of years instead of 5. Perhaps the criteria for your dream man is 6´2˝, blue eyes, blond hair, firm and toned, a nonsmoker, social drinker, owns a sailboat, has an advanced degree, and makes over $150,000 a year. You will miss anyone who is 6´1˝or below and 6´3˝ or above; has green, hazel, brown eyes, or one blue and one green. You might miss the person who puts about average for his body type and who very well might actually be firm and toned, but at his gym, he is just average. He may not wish to reveal his income and put instead "will tell you later". Any one of these examples could eliminate that special someone. However, stick firmly to your deal breakers, which are those things that you must or must not have. Examples might be such things as non-smoker, religious or ethnic preferences, recently separated and so forth. Every time that you add stringent criteria, you markedly decrease the number of fish you will see swimming in that big sea. Instead of having someone live within 20 miles of you, would you go 30 to increase your odds of meeting the right person for you? How far would you go? For instance, if you live in a small town you may have to have a larger geographical area in your search.

You can easily refine your criteria for subsequent searches. This will narrow the field to better fit what qualities you are looking for. If you narrow too much, you can always expand them to be more inclusive. So does this sound like a balancing act to you? An important aspect of marketing is to decide whom to target, should the target be large or very specific? The beauty of online dating is that it introduces you to a lot of people. Some people prefer to contact a large number of people because the attrition rate is high as many drift from your cyberspace path for whatever reasons. Wide-based targeting then might be considered to increase your chances of finding your special someone. Others favor a more selective approach, contacting fewer people who are more likely to write you back and have more in common with you. Realistically, how many people can you handle at once?

Once I emailed 6 different men at the same time and 4 of them actually emailed me back. I was turning into an email junkie and having trouble keeping up with the back and forth emailing, subsequent phone calls, and dates. I was having lunch with one man, coffee later with another, and dinner with another the next night, and another the next. This was too much time for me to spend and I had trouble keeping on schedule, keeping track of who was who, and remembering what I said to whom. I suggest that you contact fewer people, say two or three, and if this does not pan out, then you contact two or three more and so forth. Trial and error is the course on the cyberspace highway -- just take your time. Someone who is brand new to the site may initially be overwhelmed with responses and writing back later may be a better choice. But then again you have here today, gone tomorrow. There is no sure thing in dating for sure! You will find what works best for you, just keep on trying and go back to the bus stop, sooner or later (usually later) the right one will come along!

Learn all you can about the features of your online dating site, especially the search features. This can save you time, effort, and enhance your effectiveness. Several online dating sites have features where you can save your searches, see who is currently online, and reverse match you. You can even post your *hotties* or *favorites* in a special area. On some sites such as Jdate you can even see who posted you as a *favorite*. Use the "help" section and other informative areas such as a tour or map of the website.

Do not get discouraged if you only receive a few matches. You may live in an area where there are not many singles, your dating site may not have a large enough pool of singles for you, the site sends only a limited number of matches at a time, or your search is too limited. You can always sign up for an additional online dating service. However, be sure to keep them straight and know who is on first, on second and so forth. I had someone once e-mail me and say that he found me on such and such dating service, when in fact I was not on that one. This turned me off and I never replied to him. Talk about playing the field and not knowing which ballpark you are in.

Keeping track

It is important to develop some way to keep track of your contacts. You will want to begin this as soon as possible. Many sites automatically keep track of your favorites, matches, who viewed you, whom you e-mailed, and who e-mailed you back. Some link the profiles with these. However, some delete these after a specified time period. This service can be very helpful, but you need to log into the service to get this information, which is usually in various areas of the website which may require you to go to sent e-mails, and received e-mails for every one while the profile is located in another area. You also need to be in front of a computer. One system that is more portable is to print the profile of someone you wish to contact and add each e-mail to it, keeping these in a file by his or her screen name. You can jot notes down and highlight areas of special interest, and note inconsistencies and other red flags that you will need to pay close attention to.

This may strike you as quite anal and overdone, however, if you have ever looked at houses or apartments, or even cars, you quickly realize how difficult it can be to keep each one straight. The same thing happens with your contacts. Those of you who may be technologically advanced may figure out some other equally effective way such as creating separate folders for each website you are on and saving each contact's files that contain their profile and correspondence. As for myself, I'm a download, print hard copy, and file kind of gal. An example of why keeping good records is important: I called one of the men I was dating, and said, "Hi David."

His response was, "This is Don." Thank goodness they both started with D, but it was fast tap dancing for me on that one.

Contacting potential matches — Cyberflirting

Depending on the dating service you have chosen, there are various ways you can initiate contact or be contacted. Internet dating websites are constantly updating their look and adding new features. To let a person know you are interested in him or her you can select an option such as what Match. com calls a *wink* or Jdate.com refers to as a *tease*. While this allows you to be coy and indicate interest, it does not require you to put yourself on the line to reveal or say anything about yourself. This is not as effective as contacting people directly through the online dating service's e-mail or instant message. Some people do not respond to *winks* or *teases* because it takes so little effort and reveals nothing about the sender. It is best to write an initial e-mail or instant message (if that option is available) that will pique the respondent's interest and make him or her want to contact you to learn more. Your first e-mail serves as your pick-up line with the added benefit that you can design this e-mail based on information that is given to you in their profile. Ladies, do not just sit back and wait to be contacted. Let your fingers do the walking and when you spot persons of interest, do not hesitate to contact them.

Some online dating sites such as eHarmony.com provide very structured initial contacts where you select questions for someone to answer and then he or she answers them and in turn sends you some questions. You progress from short answers to questions and then to direct e-mails through the website. Both of you can decide when to go offsite to your personal e-mail or phone or in-person meeting. The matches they send you are based on the compatibility profile you completed to begin on this site. You can search outside of your matches as well.

Some sites such as Yahoo! Personals have a digital voice recorder that records a message up to thirty seconds and a digital video recorder, which requires that you have a Web cam. Others such as Match.com can also utilize your cell phone and link you anonymously with someone. This feature is not free, but it is truly anonymous.

One thing that I have found especially useful is the feature that tells you how active the person has been online. Usually this is given in terms of how recently the person has been online. Someone who has not been online for several weeks may no longer be active and has possibly quit the service and will never receive your message. This person may also have never subscribed for the service and will never receive your e-mails or be able to respond to you, yet their profile is posted to entice you and add numbers to the website. Good for them, bad for you. Another useful feature is the one that lets you know if the person is currently online and also whether you can instant message (IM) them.

Initiating contact with someone you do not know can be intimidating, confusing, and scary at first. Remember though that both men and women like when someone contacts them first. So do not hesitate for these reasons; remember that people are online to meet other people. Be active and approach persons who sound interesting to you. One word of caution here is that you should only initiate contact with people who might be interested in you. Pay attention to the criteria that they specify. For example, if they want someone who is a nonsmoker and you smoke, this may eliminate you even if you plan to quit. The same goes for someone who wants to meet persons of their own religion and race. An exception can be made for age to a certain extent because many persons state a lower age range because they expect most people to lie about it. So if the age range they list is 40-45 and you are 46 or 47, you might try. If you are over 50, this might be too big of a stretch. Do not take the criteria personally and feel bruised if the person does not reply. Some women do not wish to date someone shorter than they are and others may not be interested in riding motorcycles. So be it. This is not your match and it does not mean you are anything less than the unique being you are.

Your skill at writing good initial responses will improve with practice. It takes trial and error and your skills will increase rapidly. It is much easier to cyberflirt than to flirt in person for many of us. The following section will help you to find the right words and tone for your messages.

What shall I say in my first e-mail or instant message?

Keep it relatively short; yet provide some information about yourself and something that piqued your interest about that person from his or her profile. You want to spark the person's interest so he or she will view your profile and write back to you. You want to stand out from the pack. Take a risk and dare to be yourself: memorable and, if you can, witty. This is not the time to send an autobiography or the 10 things you have learned about life. Do NOT reveal a lot about yourself in your first e-mail, just write enough to get his or her attention and desire to write you back. Think carefully and honestly about why you want to write to this person. It might be her smile or his twinkling eyes that attracted you. If you use flattery, be sincere and specific. This by itself is a weak opener because it does not invite other conversation other than:

He: You have a great smile.

She: Thank you.

If his smile is great too, she might add the following, which will only lead to his thank you:

She: Your smile is great too

He: Thank you.

Wow, what a start, we have the possible beginning of a toothpaste ad. Seriously, compliments are nice and may indeed be very true, but where does it go from here? Oftentimes it just moves the ball into the other person's court.

If the person posted some questions in his or her profile, this is an excellent opening for you. A good first e-mail or instant message picks up on something from a posted profile, states your response, and shows a little about you. Find something that stood out in the profile, which lets the other person know that you have taken the time to read what he or she wrote, and you both have something in common. For example,

> I am impressed that the last book you read was..... I found this to be really informative and interesting, although I did not agree with everything the author said. What did you think about his viewpoint?

This example relates to something specific mentioned in his or her profile and also creates some intrigue, which invites the other party to find out what it was that you did not agree with and also to respond to your question. It is flexible enough that if the person agreed or disagreed with the book you have not made a judgment. It gives the person a conversation to follow up on with you. In this response you have focused on the reader, demonstrated interest in something about him or her, and initiated a conversation. You might find something jazzier such as:

> Hi. I think it's great that you fell in love with Paris during your visit there. It is one of my favorite cities, too. I love the museums and cafes in particular. What did you enjoy the most?"

Here is the headline and opening paragraph of someone's profile and an initial contact:

Headline: Do you believe in magic?

Opening: Life is magical... Looking for someone to join me on a magic carpet ride.

Email contact: May I ride on your magic carpet? I will bring the Pixie Dust and some magic of my own.

Be upbeat and enthusiastic in your message. Avoid being cutesy as this often backfires. Be confident. If you are playful with words, this is a great time to use humor and get a fun conversation going. It is a good idea also to counter questions with a question or two of your own. Show that you are taking the other person seriously. Do not bluff — in other words do not try to show you know something more about his or her interests or backgrounds than you do. This can often backfire and make you look fake, misinformed, or even worse, say something that gets interpreted the wrong way.

Here are some actual e-mails that my respondents or I have received. How would you respond to each of these? Which ones would you answer? Which ones turn you off? Which ones are more effective at starting a conversation?

Hi angel, How are you doing today? I read your profiles and i was realy happy with it.Well i hope that we can meet online so that we can be able to have some conversation baby,and our conversation might be compartable and have a dream to share, what a nice picture of yours with good profiles , lets start and get to know one another, the journey of one thousand miles starts with a step, who knows may be we are really match.

This email demonstrates the importance of a basic command of English grammar and spelling if you wish to attract someone who is fairly educated. If you do not wish to immerse yourself in English grammar and spelling, have dyslexia, or English is not your first language; then let your fingers do the walking and first compose your message, profile or whatever, in a basic word document. If you use Microsoft Word for Windows, go into *Tools* and use *spell check* and *grammar check*. This may seem to be a lot of work, but it is an excellent compensatory strategy for those persons who may be writing impaired. I am math impaired, and only use a calculator if I need real numbers, like for my checkbook. If you are just lazy and rush through composing an e-mail, just be aware of how you present yourself through this carelessness. Ya ain't gonna get a smart one too interested iz ya? Well, in fact, you do not have to be too smart to write better than that and recognize illiteracy.

> I read your profile and liked what I read. It sounds as if you are spunky and I like that. I love to travel and want to meet a woman who likes the kind of active adventures you describe and who has an upbeat attitude toward life. I am a lawyer, too. If you could change one thing in the world, what would that be?

> Enjoyed reading about all the things you like to do. I have approximately the same list, but add: gardening and boating. I just moved to <deleted>, bought a house in <deleted>. Boat at my dock in the backyard. Based on what I read in your profile: I would appreciate an opportunity to get to know you. Please let me know your thoughts. Thanks for reading this.

Great photos! As a legman, your photos don't display much. :-). If my profile is at all interesting, let me know and photos will follow.

This is the line from your profile that caught my attention... .

He goes on here to quote my statement of what I consider to be some of my most characteristic traits and ended up with a zinger of a question that of course I wanted to answer because it was about me and something that I was interested in talking about.

I really like your smile and your profile sounds very interesting. It sounds as if we have several things in common. Please read my profile and if you are interested in contacting me, I would like the opportunity to learn more about you. Will you give me the opportunity?

The previous e-mail could be a bit more specific about what sounds so interesting from the profile, but all in all is not a bad initial contact. The question does not particularly lend itself to an answer other than yes or no. Do you find that it grabs you and makes you want to respond? Here are two more to think about:

Call me at 333-977-0000. We should talk.

We obviously have a lot in common. I believe that you'd both complement and enhance my life. Whether I might do the same for you, you'll have to decide. Want to talk? My phone number is... .

Telling someone in an introductory email to "Call me.

We should talk." really says, "I really do not want to put too much effort into this." This person often uses the shotgun approach — send out lots of small bits in the hope that someone will call. This is another reason why picking up specific things from someone's profile is much better because it is personal and therefore likely to get an answer. Neither of the last two emails accomplishes this and are totally generic.

You want to be sure that you do not give out your phone number in your initial emails because once you give it up, you cannot get it back. You do not want to give it to someone you do not know enough about. Even if you have a writing phobia, hate to write, or have carpal tunnel syndrome, do not succumb to premature telephonation. Not only does this violate your anonymity, but also it should be earned. Do not be so easy. Guys particularly like to get out of writing and on to the phone quickly. This is premature telephonation and gals, make him wait until you are good and ready. If he stops e-mailing you because he does not want to write and wants to get right down to hearing your voice, this may be a good red flag to pay attention to. It says, "me want and me want it now". This guy is not about to delay gratification and genuinely give what is needed for a relationship to work. Hold on to your self-respect and what you are really looking for. I cannot stress this enough. Take it slow and easy.

Here is an initial email to a guy, whose profile says that he coaches Little League baseball; is 6'1" tall; loves his dog, Buster, who once won a Frisbee contest, and is looking for someone special to run with him and Buster and share life's joys.

Hi Coach.

Your profile is great and I cannot resist responding to it possibly because I am looking for an athletic dog whose owner also runs. Can you catch a Frisbee as well as your dog can? My Lhasa Apso is a wonderful dog, but with her short legs and her regal disposition, a run to the end of my driveway is enough for her; but not for me. May I try out for your team?

The response above demonstrates several of the characteristics of a good initial email. First of all it is warm and personal. It does not sound as if it could have been written to anyone else. It is short yet contains enough information to start a conversation. The "Hi Coach" is an eye-catching subject heading that picks up on some specific information from his profile. People glance at their e-mail lists and look at the subject heading usually before opening an email. An initial e-mail should use a catchy subject heading. Do not waste this opportunity to stand out from the pack. It explains what attracted you to the person instead of all the others on the website and what makes him or her special. End your e-mail with a warm and pressure-free closing. Compare the example above with this too generic one:

What a great profile! You sound very interesting. Please check out my profile and if interested, please write me back.

Hello, hello are you there?

Now you have completed the hardest part and it is easy

to just sit back and hope for the mail to pour in and your soul mate to find you. Instead, actively use the Internet as a dating tool to get the results you want, which does take time. What is important is that you go to the bus stop and sooner or later the right bus is likely to come along. This is why you cannot give up the search and allow yourself time and opportunity to meet the right one. It is easy to become frustrated and opt out. New singles are coming online all the time and while you are looking, you are improving your skills and becoming even clearer about what you want, as well as what you do not. Usually people remain active online until they meet someone and then cancel their subscription. If this relationship ends, they sign up again on the same or another site.

People who do not fall madly in love within a few months often become discouraged and quit as do people who have a bad experience. A rejection makes some people run for cover. It is more productive instead to take a good long look at yourself. There is always some way to improve your profile, your photographs, your e-mails or a whole approach that might be undermining your efforts. Do not take the easy way out and retreat or resign yourself to lurking around the website but not subscribing or not contacting others. Instead, examine yourself as objectively as you can. What is your pattern? What impression do you give? Ask others how they see your profile, what you write, what you say, and what you do. Women, times have changed and it is fine to contact men, in fact, they like it. This does not mean that you are desperate or aggressive; it simply indicates that you are interested, which is good. Men, just like women, like to have someone indicate an interest in them. Many men report that they receive lots of e-mails and just keeping up with these is enough and they do not search for additional women. Yes, all right so they may be popular and the competition is stiff; but if you do not play, how can you win? Your chances are markedly better than the lottery! Get your foot in the door. Here is what one man had to say:

> I subscribed to this online dating service and within the first week had over 30 emails. There was no way I could or would even want to contact everyone. I first deleted those women without photographs, poorly written or bland profiles, and women who did not match the characteristics that I was looking for. This left me with 7 potential dates. I marked 4 of these as "favorites" and emailed the other 3. I ended up casually dating two of the women and the third woman lost interest in me. About 6 weeks later I received an email from a woman who sounded very interesting and said that my profile spoke to her because... . I e-mailed her back. We have been dating for about a year and have a great relationship. I would not have met her if she had not e-mailed me. In fact, the only women I have met online have contacted me first.

So women, take heed and take thy mouse into thy paw and write Mr. Good Stuff. You can bet that your competition is doing just that!

SAFETY CYBERSMARTS

Although online dating services have numerous advantages and will expose you to many quality singles, there are undesirables out there as well with whom you are likely to come in contact. It is imperative that you develop cybersmarts and protect your privacy until you feel safe enough to let the person contact you off the dating site. Just as in any type of dating, you must be careful. You want to be confident and positive, yet remain aware and protect yourself just in case.

Protect Your Anonymity

While you are communicating within the online dating services, anonymity exists in that everyone is referred to by his or her screen name. Reputable services do not release any identifiable information about you to other members. Again, remember to select a screen name that is not your full name or that identifies you.

Do not include any mention of your real e-mail address in your online dating service e-mails. Get a special e-mail account for yourself that you use exclusively for your online dating free from websites such as www.yahoo.com or www.hotmail.com or MSN.com or earthlink.com. Use your screen name or some variation for this e-mail account; do not use your real name or anything else that might identify you. This is one you keep exclusively for your online dating adventures to protect your anonymity. If you have subscribed to more than one online dating service, then you will need separate accounts for each one. You do not want to confuse who is from where. You can give out your real name and e-mail address when you are good and ready and feel safe doing so. Once you give it out and find it to be a mistake, it can be a big hassle. You do not want to have to change your phone number, regular e-mail and so forth. Once someone has your name and number, you are easy to find.

It is not uncommon for someone to ask you for an e-mail address for several reasons: 1) to send you additional photographs that they do not wish to post online or that give you more of a sense of their life space. I had a man send me delightful digital pictures of a sunrise he just saw, the view of the ocean from his condominium, the houses on a garden tour he took that day and so forth. These were beautiful and also gave me much more of a sense of him. 2) To get your real name and how to contact you. You avoid this by getting an anonymous email service as previously described. 3) Some persons do not want to pay for the online service and want to just contact you directly. Also be sure that your offsite e-mail does not contain an automatic signature at the end. Certain e-mail addresses also can be searched to find you. For example, if your email address is johndoe@csu.edu you can be found by searching Colorado State University's website. *edu* refers to an educational institution just as *com* refers to a commercial business, *org* refers to an organization, and *gov* refers to government. These are not good e-mails to use for offsite dating. Besides, your employer may be watching!

Your contact may tell you that it is too much of a bother to go online to the dating site. He or she may tell you that he or she is going out of town and will not have access to the website. Hey, now wait a minute here. Many of the major sites send your messages to offsite e-mail that you give them as well. This offsite e-mail sends you your e-mails and matches, too without you having to log in to the dating site. Also, to get most e-mail, you need to go onto the Internet anyway. If you have web e-mail this really does not make any sense. Oops, there is an exception because I actually did venture to Africa and I had very limited and expensive Internet access and therefore did not go online at all. In any case, for some reason the person wants to go outside of the service. One of the more understandable reasons is to be able to send each other additional photographs. This is when your special offsite e-mail address is very useful. I do not understand why so many persons prefer to be contacted offsite when this usually happens automatically anyway.

You can block your caller ID to protect your anonymity. Phone numbers can be traced back to your name. It is not necessary to get an unlisted number, just block the caller ID function as described later in the **Call me** section. You can also use a pre-paid phone card that goes through the phone company service line, not yours.

If someone is pressing you for personal information, this should raise a red flag and it is best to express that you are not comfortable giving this information at this time. If he or she continues to pressure you, then cease communication immediately. This is not someone who respects your wishes and boundaries.

Take your cell phone with you when you go to meet someone and be sure that it is a public place that you are familiar with when you meet someone for the first time. Have an exit strategy in mind if needed. Also let a friend or roommate know where you are going and who this person is just in case.

Do not let him pick you up at your home

Definitely do not let him or her pick you up at your home for the first meeting and then not until you feel safe and that he or she is trustworthy. First of all, you are just meeting this person and you need to be careful whom you allow into your home, which of course you know. Second, when a man (also could apply to women) drives and picks his date up at home, he has to bring him or her home and this gives him a better opportunity to make his sexual moves. Once someone is in your house, it is harder to get them out and awkward situations could arise.

Checking in

Make sure your friends know where you are going, with whom, and when you expect to be home. Take a cell phone with you and have it on you at all times; borrow one if you do not have one and be sure the phone is fully charged. You may want to call your babysitter if you have one to check in.

Trust your gut reaction

Be cautious of someone who seems too good to be true. Keep looking for inconsistencies and contradictions. This person may not be whom he or she says. Pay attention to your gut-level feeling. Proceed very slowly and walk away if anything makes your uncomfortable. Let us analyze the following **first** email a woman received:

> Will be in your area next weekend and why don't we plan on having lunch Saturday and then hit the spa for a good massage? That will be our introduction and perhaps on my next trip day we can plan something else. I will be on my way to race a sailboat in _____ __that next week and not sure when I will get back your way. I promise you will find me handsome, interesting, and full of life.

What is your gut reaction? Does this first email strike you as somewhat unusual? Does it entice you by mentioning a massage and get you to wondering if he is going to pay for it? From my own experience and that of others this is quite an unusual way for people to meet for the first time. It elicited an uncomfortable gut reaction. Logically, how do people get to know each other in a spa receiving a massage? She checked out his profile for more clues and found that he sought to meet women whenever he traveled to a race and found this to be quite adventurous and what he was looking for. He also lived with his parents. She could not stifle herself from responding:

> Hi. Let me see if I got your message right. You are a traveling sailorman looking for a good time in ports on your way to sailing races. You want to meet for lunch and then do a spa massage. Although I love massages, I do not understand how a spa massage fits in. Fly by night guys are not my cup of tea and not what I am looking for.

This man may be sincere and not Jack the Ripper, but is this the type of encounter that you are looking for and want to risk? Is it worth your precious time?

Block that pass

If you receive an e-mail that is out of line, offensive, or in any other way disagreeable you can report the concern to the online dating service and block that person from contacting you again. You may wish to check for these features before you select a service. I had a man in his twenties contact me stating, "I like older women." Just to be smart (but not cybersmart) I e-mailed him back "I preferred older men." Not so smart on my part after all. He then emailed me explicitly comparing his sexual prowess to that of older men. I immediately blocked and deleted him. He is out there somewhere in cyberspace, but no longer in my cyberspace. The cybersmart move would have been to immediately block and delete him since I was not looking for a fling with a much younger man. I am not a *cougar*, which is a term used to describe an older woman who is looking for sex with a much younger man. Most online dating services do not screen e-mail between members and have a disclaimer for liability. Many also have a place to report abuse, and something like this should be reported. Do not put up with this type of behavior, unless of course you really are a *cougar* and are looking for a frolic with a much younger fellow who is not really big on the niceties of pre-foreplay and wants to get right to the action.

Scams

Unfortunately scams happen on dating sites, too. I have heard from a few men that some women online are really ladies of the night who find this a great way to advertise their services. Then there are those looking for a ticket to America or money or both. A sad example of this is:

> He was a widower in his 60s and lonely and wanted a wife. There were few single women where he lived and he found it hard to go out and meet women. He received an email from a beautiful young woman in Russia. They corresponded and decided to meet and then probably marry. She lacked the money to come to America and meet him, clothes, and loss of time from work, the sick mother, and all the rest. He sent her $5000 to cover expenses so that she could make the trip. He never heard from her again.

What a hard way to become older and wiser! Several men have reported variations of this scam.

Stalkers and Lurkers

Stalkers are usually very insecure people who cannot handle rejection. They may resort to stalking while in a relationship because they anticipate and fear rejection. Once a relationship ends, they do not exit gracefully and move on. They may follow you, often suddenly appear at places where you are, call in the middle of the night, sit in their car in front of your house for hours, and so forth. This usually freaks the stalked one out because of its *Fatal Attraction* overtones. Stalkers are not unique to online dating and you can meet them anywhere.

Lurkers are those persons online who write rather unusual profiles and usually do not post pictures of themselves. You notice them if your online dating site has the feature that lets you view the profiles of persons who viewed you. They constantly appear, yet they do not contact you. Why do they keep lurking around in the background and not contact you? I certainly do not know, but I have found it to be rather creepy and have blocked these persons from being able to view me.

Your best protection from these persons is to keep your anonymity and then you can block the person or report the suspicious behavior to the website. Keep any of the lewd, threatening or weird e-mails and forward them to the online dating company. The company is limited in what it can do and usually may throw the person off the site. However, he or she can reappear as someone else. So another word of caution here is that if you meet someone who is not the same person as the photo in the profile, leave—do not pass Go. Do not collect $200, just go—disappear as fast as you can.

When dealing with stalkers or lurkers you do not want to do anything that would encourage them—which means giving them your attention. You must ignore them, which does not reinforce their behavior and cease all communication immediately. Ignore them when they appear and do not peek out the window at them sitting in their car at your curb, literally or virtually. Nada, nothing, that is unless the behavior is in any way threatening. Then you can save any correspondence, keep notes, get witnesses and report it to the police. If this is not enough, a restraining order might be needed to protect you from serious harm. In all of my interviews with online daters, I have not heard of a restraining order being necessary, but have heard of it in response to people who met in more traditional ways, such as a bar. This is not to say that it does not happen online as well.

CHECKING THEM OUT

Some people go one step further and check the person out in a wide variety of ways on line. Once you have the person's name you can search www.google.com or www.yahoo.com. Simply type the person's name in the search section. It is best if you have a middle name or initial, especially if the name is a common one. You may find news articles, press releases, and other information mentioning them. You will find many sites that will give you people's addresses, phone numbers, birth dates, aerial photographs of their homes, criminal checks and background searches. Some of these include www.peopledata.com, www.ussearch.com, and www.privateeye.com. Some are free and others have a fee depending on the depth of information that you wish. You can also check to see if someone is a licensed professional for free on line by checking those websites for the particular state you are in. The more sophisticated you get with searches, the more information you can find. Check yourself out and see what you find.

No, Thanks

For whatever reasons, you may not be interested in pursuing contact with some people and you can say this in a way that is not rude or insulting or damaging to their self-esteem. It is not necessary for you to give a lecture to the person if their words, views and so forth are offensive. You may feel better, but the recipient probably will not read it and will think you are a little over the top and disqualify you and label you one of those *libbers, tree-huggers, men haters, chauvinist pigs,* etc. If there is a specific reason, you might wish to give a brief response that does not attack them as a person but gives some insight, which does not leave them wondering what is wrong with them. You also do **not** need to justify your position. Here are examples.

> Hi. Thank you for writing me. You are right that we have a lot in common. However, I do not date women who are separated or recently divorced. From my past experiences, there is too much baggage for me to handle. I wish you luck in your search.

> Hi. Thank you for contacting me. You sound delightful but I do not think we share the same interests. I am not into motorcycles or skiing. Best wishes in your search for the right one.

> Thank you for emailing me, but the distance is too great for me to explore a relationship with you.

In this last one, you are "GU" (geographically undesirable).

Many persons are looking for someone local and distance is a definite factor to them. It is also interesting to note that many persons report hearing from people all over the world.

Here is a generic response for someone who just does not light any fires or sound like someone you are looking for:

> Thank you for emailing me, but I do not think that we are a good match. I wish you luck in your search. You sound like you have a lot to offer the right person.

You may also think, "No, thanks" about someone who does not put effort into their e-mails to you. You may have asked questions that were not answered, were scantily addressed, or lacked some commentary about what you said. For whatever reasons: he or she has too many emails to attend to, is unable to articulate well, has no sense of humor, is self-centered, is not that in to you, or this person does not demonstrate the ability and/or desire to make an effort with you. Why then continue with someone like this? You may give them a few e-mails to see if this changes or you may just cut to the chase and quit. In this case, "No, thanks" is best handled by not responding back to them. Why continue to spend more effort with someone who does not? You are giving a lot more than you are receiving right from the get-go.

YES

Ah, you have received a contact from someone you want to get to know better. Yes, this does happen and it is fun! This is the place to use your best conversation skills and if what you have isn't so terrific — work on them. You will need to have these skills for most aspects of successful living. There are many books and information available online that deal with the art of conversation. Basically a conversation is a two-way flow of communication between a sender and receiver. There is give and take: the sender and receiver alternate roles. A conversation is not all about you, nor all about them. Here are some responses that keep the conversation going after the first e-mail exchange.

Hi, I am delighted that you wrote me back and yes, in response to your question, I would like to continue getting to know more about you. You have a great sense of humor and I liked what you said in response to my question about your family and values. They are very similar to mine. I also have two children, Maggie, who is 8 and wants to try out for every team boys play on, and Kevin, whose computer, I fear, has become a permanent part of his body at the tender age of 11. I have to email him to tell him it's dinnertime. I agree that parenthood is a serious responsibility and full of daily challenges. You sound like a great parent who also enjoys children as much as I do. What do you enjoy doing most with your children and what is the hat game you said you all play? When I have free time I often curl up with a good book and listen to smooth jazz. In fact, I just finished reading the book you listed as one of your favorites.

As I said earlier, online dating gives you some information about the person with which to start. It is much easier to initiate and respond to a conversation when you have some areas to pick up on and you are starting slower than with traditional dating. You are feeling each other out as you decide whether or not to continue contacting each other. The e-mail above shows that the individuals took the time to continue to construct personal and specific emails that are conversational and have a give and take flow. The person's initial response asked questions that made the other's response easier. Each of them revealed something about themselves both in response to questions and volunteered. Yet, neither of them made the conversation all about them. They created a dialog, which is so much different than a diatribe! This is also much different than when someone responds with only answers to your questions. Where do you go from there? Will you ask more questions or give your answer to the questions even if this was not asked for? You were not given much back to go on. You may have to go back to the profile or response and try a different approach to get a dialog going or look further to find someone more interested in you. So be sure that you do not do this in your conversations with others. If you cannot communicate with the person in an e-mail, how will you be able to communicate on the phone or on a date with him or her? Remember to write as you speak to keep it conversational and characteristic of you. Sincerity, depth, humor and creativity are important. Curt responses give an abrupt impression and will not differentiate you from your competitors. E-mail responses have the advantage that you can take time to develop your response. You can think about how the person will receive your message. You can write, edit, re-edit, delete, and so forth until the e-mail is actually sent. Content should be positive, upbeat, and fairly light at this stage in the online dating game. Unless you are looking for sex and are on a sexually oriented site, keep talk about sex light and flirty. If you say something sexual, think about if it can be taken in the wrong way. If so, it is best not to send it because the other person may not think it is funny and that you are weird or brash or coming on too strong sexually and goodbye to you.

In successful conversations the receiver accurately perceives the message as intended by the sender. However, miscommunication often happens and it is important to clear up. Saying such things as "Did I understand you correctly to say...?" or "I'm not sure I understand what you meant by.... Would you clarify that for me?" Choice of wording is very important here. A curt or sarcastic e-mail gives these statements a much different meaning than a sincere question or statement. So watch your wording, and on the phone watch your tone! Also remember not to talk too much about yourself; your conversation should be a dialog, not a monologue. Do not monopolize the conversation and remember not to go on and on with too much information (TMI).

Do I answer on the first ring?

Once you decide to respond to an e-mail, how soon should you answer it? You do not want to sound too eager, nor do you want to let the opportunity go by and appear disinterested. Generally it is best to answer the following day and if someone does not answer in a few days, then they are probably not interested or you are put on their wait list. Nowadays, most people check their emails everyday or so; if they are interested, but busy attending a conference, meeting with the Pope, or going where no Internet has ever been, they will usually tell you that in a brief email and indicate they will get back to you as soon as they return in a specific time frame.

The problem with e-mail is that it is insynchronous in that, unlike the telephone or chat, you are carrying on a conversation with time lags between each of your responses. We have come to expect rapid responses to e-mail and short time lags between. Therefore if both of you are online at the same time and instant messaging or emailing back and forth you often get a nice rhythm going. You appear interested and enthusiastic as well, which is much different from too eager. You have a conversation going with less lengthy pauses. Do not overload him or her with e-mails and wait for a response before you answer, unless you have something short and quick to say right now. Remember the goal is to have a 2-way conversation where you explore more about each other to see if each of you wants to continue.

Another school of thought is for online daters, especially women, to play it more aloof and make the other person work for attention. Supposedly this makes one more appealing and different from the others who may be rushing her. His or her unavailability or cool demeanor creates intrigue, which increases interest. This school of hard-to-get may appeal to some but can easily become a game. I recommend that you respond sincerely in a timely manner with the best response you can muster.

Other views recommend that you try to meet the person as soon as you can to see if you have any chemistry. Many persons, especially men, seem to like this approach and they explained to me that chemistry is essential for any romantic relationship to work and they wanted to find out as soon as possible whether or not it was there. I call this the "cut to the chase" approach. I recommend not rushing to speak on the phone or meet for a date until some e-mail conversation has ensued that naturally leads to these next steps and both you and the other party feel comfortable. This gives you time to learn a bit more about each other and break the ice, which may smooth the way for you. It is important to establish that you are able to talk with each other and enjoy it first. This certainly does not debunk the importance of chemistry at all, but points out that it does not hurt to slow down a bit and e-mail and talk on the phone a few times before deciding to meet. Yes, just a few times of each, which is not an extensive amount of time to spend. Your date may be more enjoyable if you have conversed with the person a bit before you decide to meet. This also will help you to further weed out those persons with characteristics that do not light your fire or discover additional stellar aspects of the other party.

If this is a long-distance romance, you definitely will want to establish trust and a feeling of comfort and compatibility with the other person before you decide to meet. This will involve considerably more phone conversations and sharing each of yourselves. When someone travels a long distance to meet you or vice-versa, this is not usually a two- or three- hour date. You are likely to spend a good deal of time together for at least a day or two depending upon the distance. This puts a lot of pressure on that first meeting and magnifies the expense, time spent in enjoyment or thinking "How many more hours until this is over? I cannot wait until he or she leaves." The visit also may pose other awkward problems, especially if one of you stays at the other's home. One's privacy is invaded and you do not want a stranger learning private things about you that your home reveals. The other person is out of his or her familiar territory and is your guest, which can be uncomfortable for him or her. Meeting somewhere neutral can be even more uncomfortable for both of you. So slow down, develop a relationship first and keep your expectations down. I have heard numerous stories of people who did not meet for at least two months and when they finally met, felt that they knew a great deal about each other from the many hours of talking on the phone and sharing. For many, meeting was the icing on the cake, which led to marriage or long-term significant relationships.

Second base--continuing offsite

Call me

Sooner or later one of you will ask the other to begin contact off the dating site, either by another e-mail address or by phone. Some sites such as Match.com have a feature that can hook you up by phone anonymously for a fee. Men seem particularly more prone to seek phone contact very early in the conversation. Reasons that men have given include their dislike of writing, wanting to hear a real person's voice, and belief that you can tell so much more about a person on the phone. Usually men will give a woman their phone number and ask her to call them. Hey, gals, this is not the time to say, "I don't call men. I wait for them to call me." This is the 21st century and also in online dating, the rules are different. Men, just as women, like to be called. Men offer the woman their phone number in a chivalrous gesture so that the choice is hers and they do not put her in a position where she is asked to reveal her number. Of course with caller ID and other means of identification, you reveal this when you call back unless you take preemptory measures to block your caller ID. You can avoid revealing your name and number on a call by several means. A cell phone rarely reveals your name and is not listed in the white pages; some cell phones companies even have a caller ID blocking system. You can always block your landline caller ID and number by finding out how your phone service does this, which usually is by dialing a specific code. Beware, 800 and 877 numbers are very difficult to block. Calling from your office phone is not usually any better and

F. LUDWIG

has another set of problems of its own.

So with all this said, eventually one of you decides to seek offline contact and offer the other an alternative. What happens then depends on the comfort level of the other person and his or her gut reaction. Many of us, especially women, are anxious and shy about talking to someone we have not met or know little about on the phone. This is not a good reason by itself to refuse. This is a social skill that you need to develop and use even when you first meet someone in person. Have you ever given out your phone number to someone you just met and know very little about? If something does not feel right go with that feeling and ask them to continue onsite for a while longer. You might include the following in your response:

> I am more comfortable emailing a bit more before we talk in person.

You do not have to offer a reason. Follow your statement with a question or comment to keep the e-mail conversation going. If the other person refuses, then this tells you something very important...and that is a very good indication how he or she will handle your wishes and consideration of you! Exit stage right!

Indicators that may help you decide that you are ready to talk on the phone are: 1) what he or she says and does in the profile and in contacts with you has been consistent 2) you have some feel for him or her as a person with some integrity, 3) you want to learn more and a telephone conversation will add to that, and 4) you can maintain your cybersmart safety.

A word of caution here about what might happen if you give your cell phone number to someone or you call someone on his or her cell phone. Very simply, he or she can be anywhere doing anything when the cell phone rings.

> They emailed a bit and then he gave her his cell phone number and asked her to call him. She did and he answered, sounded a bit uncomfortable, asked her if he could call her back later, he was in a bar talking with a woman.

She wondered why he even answered his cell phone in those circumstances. How rude to the other woman he was talking to and this was also a turn-off for her.

Third base

Let's meet

So you have emailed each other, talked on the phone, and now want to meet in person. This is much better than a blind date because you know some things about each other, yet a lot of mystery remains. Does he or she really look like he or she said? Is he or she 10 years older than the pictures and 40 pounds more? What will we talk about? Will I be stuck for hours talking with someone who is boring...boring... boring? Is she going out with me only for a free dinner? And the foremost question, will there be chemistry between us? These are a few of the questions that go through almost everyone's head. It happens, it's real...but get over it and just do it. Develop a mindset that you will have a good time regardless. You can learn something from almost everyone and more about yourself. Just do not let your expectations for the evening get out of hand. In the Common Mistakes section of this book, I discuss more about this huge problem of expectations. Visualize having a good time learning about someone else and this is more likely to happen.

Where to meet? That one is easy…in a very public place that you are familiar with. Also remember the tips given in the **Cybersmarts** section. Should the first meeting in person be short and sweet such as for coffee or a drink or longer for lunch or dinner? Some people prefer that the first meeting be short to determine if there is a spark or as many say "chemistry" and desire to see more of each other. If not, less time and money have been invested. Others feel dinner or lunch is a good initial meeting especially if they have enjoyed talking with the person on the phone. Other clever fellows that I have met opted for a drink in the early evening and if things went well, we continued with dinner.

Ladies, it is good manners to offer to split the bill for the first date, which shows you are not a *foodie,* who is a person only out for a free meal. Men have reported a number of experiences with women who fit the term. Who pays is a loaded topic with differing opinions. Traditional gender roles have been called into question as women have claimed more independence, choice, and equality. Men are truly confused about what women want and women differ widely in what they chose to be equal and independent about. A woman may call a man, ask him out, and still expect him to pay for the date. Other women insist on splitting the check to claim their equality while others insist on paying for the check to assert their power and not owe the man anything. How is the poor fellow to know how she feels about paying and what might really offend her? Some women will not go out again with a man who lets her pay or split the bill, while others will be offended by his paying and robbing her of her independence. Many women consider a man cheap if he lets her pay. Another school of thought says that the one who initiated the date should pay while an alternative thought is that the bill should be split. Hmmm, lots of choices here and no wonder this is confusing. In order to diminish the costs of time and money, some people make the first meeting one for coffee or a drink, which is not very romantic, but an effective way to meet. Others prefer a more romantic type of first encounter over lunch or dinner. In this case, I recommend that the woman offer to split the bill. A gentleman who is not cheap preferably will then say, "Thank you, but I'll get it this time." If she insists again, then the man should let her pay because she is probably not interested in him and does not want to be indebted to him or she is demonstrating her power.

Do not talk only about yourself. Be interested in and ask your date about him -or her-self. Women often complain that men talk only about themselves and rarely ask questions. Ask, be genuinely interested, and remember the answers.

You have or are working on good conversation skills and almost anybody has something to say. If the person is drunk, on drugs, inappropriate, or rude and offensive, you should leave. Of course you came in your own car and can leave at any time. Luckily these characters and incidents are very rare.

VANISHED, INTO THIN AIR

One of the big mysteries of any type of dating is when the other party vanishes into thin air. This occurs often for both men and women at any point in some relationships. He or she may *wink, flirt,* or e-mail you indicating his or her interest. You e-mail back what you think is a great introductory email and never hear from him or her again. You are left scratching your head; you go back and read the message you sent and have absolutely no clue why you did not get a response. You followed the advice in this book and yet not a second glance. Someone else comes on really strong and you meet and feel a real chemistry and interest between you and again all you get at best is "I'll call you." The call never comes. Again you feel confused and wonder, "What did I miss, this seemed like a wonderful evening to me and we clicked." There are so many reasons this could happen that I urge you again: **do not take this personally.** There are many reasons that he or she did not call back, especially in the early stages of a relationship. Perhaps the connection was not so strong as you felt, perhaps you reminded him or her a former spouse, perhaps he or she was receiving 5-10 e-mails a day and was busy trying to sort this out, or he or she got cold feet, or whatever. Do not let your fear of rejection overwhelm you, put you in a funk, and stop you from making good decisions and taking reasonable risks.

Forget about it! Move on. There are more fish in the sea

and it is time to get back in the boat without adding this to your baggage or weighing down your self-esteem. If you have been online for anytime at all, you have probably vanished down the rabbit hole from some people yourself. Timing, timing, timing also is important as the following examples illustrate:

> I had been e-mailing back and forth with a charming man just before we had a nasty hurricane in Florida. He emailed me again after asking how I weathered the hurricane. He asked if I was ready to meet him in person or did I wish to e-mail him some more. Considerate fellow! He also lived about 60 miles away. I do not recall which of us went down the rabbit hole first, but as interesting as it sounded, I think both of us were just too worn out after the hurricane to muster up the energy.

> A man initiated contact with an interesting-sounding woman who matched his interests well. He e-mailed her and got back the response, "My mother died yesterday and I will not be dating for a while." For the next month he looked to see if she was back online and she had not been. About 5 weeks later she was back online, but it was not with him. For whatever reasons, she did not go back to her previous e-mails with him and who knows if with anyone else.

Of course in these two examples, there is no harm in e-mailing that person again at what could be better timing.

What about e-mailing someone again who has not responded to you at all? Well, you can try again, but not again and again and again. She said:

> His profile blew me away. We matched in almost every way. I could not believe my great fortune. I e-mailed

him with the great news that we were a match and clicked in so many areas. I never heard from him. I could not believe that this could not excite him, too. What was wrong with him? Couldn't he recognize his soul mate? So I waited two weeks and e-mailed him a great response with examples of our commonalities, and so forth. I received an impersonal short e-mail from him thanking me for contacting him and how busy he was and that I sounded great, and he would get back to me. That was a month ago and I have not heard from him.

Her e-mails to him were great and right on target, but for some reason or another she did not ring his chimes. You cannot beat someone over the head to become involved with you. Hopefully, during this time she did not put all of her eggs in his basket and build a fantasy that this man was her soul mate.

HOME RUN

At this point, you have met, decided to pursue a relationship and start dating. Some signs that this is a good match are: 1) you constantly find things that you want to share with each other, 2) you discover quirky things or habits that you have in common, 3) your friends can see you together and like him or her, 4) you understand what each other are saying and miscommunication does not happen frequently, 5) you laugh a lot with each other, and 6) each of you can be your real self around the other. I have also found that my dog is a great detector of good people. She warms up readily to kindhearted genuine people. During one date she gave her opinion by defecating next to his feet. She caught on quicker than I did.

My job guiding you through the cruising and bruising of the adventure of online dating is almost over, but not until I cover two more extremely important topics: 1) common mistakes and 2) set your radar for these bruisers. These are two very important sections to read and I hope that our experiences will help you avoid them or at least recognize them sooner.

Common Mistakes

Yee gads, I'm addicted!

- You find yourself making a lame excuse why you cannot go out with your office workers for a celebratory drink after work
- Your phone at work rings, but you cannot stop to answer it because you cannot stop what you are doing
- If you are still on a dial-up Internet connection that you also use for a phone line, no one is able to get through to you because your phone is always busy.
- You are behind at work because you are using your computer to do other things
- You often miss dinner or lunch
- Time passes and you do not even notice
- You get a rush when you see that you received e-mail
- You trip over your dog as you rush to the phone to see who called
- You have conducted over 15 searches that day
- It is 7 PM and you still haven't brushed your teeth or gotten dressed for the day
- It is 2 AM and you are still actively online even though you have to get up at 6 AM

- Your home page on your computer is your online dating site and it is always on
- You recognize other people who are also on other websites
- You recognize when someone has changed websites
- You don't have time to go to the gym anymore
- You do not have time for your friends
- You are going out every night of the week
- You have multiple dates in one day

If you find that you are doing any of the above because you are online searching for dating prospects, have to see if you got any new e-mails within the past few hours, or anything else related to online dating, yes my friend, you are indeed addicted. Online dating should come with the warning: **Online dating can be hazardous to your health and life in general.** If you are on Match.com, check into Dr. Phil's advice section. Instead of going cold turkey you may need to set some limits on how far you will let yourself succumb to the temptation to be an online junkie.

Not ending a relationship soon enough

Oh, the reasons for not ending a relationship soon enough, let me count several of the ways.

He or she is nice, but...

There is no chemistry. She's a great person and we share so much in common, but there is no spark.

He's really nice, but he is so narrowly focused. All he cares to talk about is.... and.... . I enjoy those things a lot, but he fixates on those topics and of course his work. He is deeply intense about them, but it ends there.

It's better than nothing

It may be better than nothing, but it is not something that sustains and nourishes you. So you ask yourself, "If I give this up, will I be home alone, have no one to go out with? You cannot have it all." This type of reasoning is defeating and caters to your worst fears and feelings of abandonment and loneliness. "It's better than nothing" keeps you from finding that something. Even if you think you are looking around and doing double duty by dating the better-than-nothing person, you are not really serving either of you well.

Ignoring red flags

You have ignored any of the red flags mentioned so far and in this chapter and in Set Your Radar For These. You doubted your gut reaction and you were overly generous in giving him or her the benefit of the doubt. Some of us, especially me at first, had to be hit over the head before we finally learned and the important thing is not to make the same mistake twice. If you are going to make mistakes as we all do, be creative and do not make the same ones again and again.

There's someone better

This is the other side of the coin from not ending a relationship soon enough. You are caught up in the swirl of so many men (women), so little time. You see how many interesting people are online and you are busy searching, sending, receiving e-mails and dating. This can naturally make you think that there is someone better out there. The problem with getting caught up in this flurry of activity and type of thinking is that you do not give the relationships a chance to develop. You are on a merry-go-round of chasing after the love of your life and going round and round and never getting anywhere. You have a good relationship going with someone, but discontent is always there because you have fallen victim to the belief that there is someone better out there just cruising along in cyberspace. Your good relationship cannot survive such thinking.

Letting him or her into your house too soon

What can I tell you about this mistake that you might not already imagine? Yes, your home is your sanctuary, it is hopefully a place you feel safe. Why let a stranger or someone your hardly know into it? Let me count the ways to discourage you, first of all, safety. He or she could be a wolf in sheep's clothing. Oh yes, this has happened to several persons who discussed their experiences with me. The person comes to your home and seems nice enough, but then the sexual advances begin. The person could also be terribly annoying, or someone with whom you do not match. Once in, how do you get him or her out? For example:

They emailed back and forth several times and then progressed to telephone conversations. They each had dogs and decided to meet for the first time at the dog park at 3:00. At 2:30 he called her and said that he was running some errands in her neighborhood and was running late and would not have time to run home and get his dog. He asked if instead he could pick her up at her house since he was in the neighborhood and they would figure out something else to do. Being the nice (but not cybersmart) girl she said yes. To make a long tiring story short, he started talking and she had a terrible time getting him to leave. She politely (because she was nice) said, "Would you like to go out and get some coffee?" He said, "No, I am having such a good time here, let's stay here and talk and get to know each other better." He talked on and on. She desperately tried to remember what she learned in assertive training but did not use it. She finally stated, "I promised my Dad I would be at his place at 7. I have to go now." He kept on talking. Finally she decided not to be so nice, which was a bit easier now, because he was so insensitive and rude. She got up, headed for the door and said, "Let's go, I have to leave now." She opened the door and fixed her eyes on him until he finally got up and headed out the door with her many hours later.

Now had this woman been quicker and responded assertively, this unpleasant situation could have been avoided. She simply could have said at the start when he asked if he could pick her up at her house, "There is a coffee shop right near here. Let's meet there." This is a good assertive response that respects both of them and follows the wise rule of meeting someone first in a familiar public place. If she was not so invested in being *nice*, they would have met for a shorter time and decided this was not a good match. By being *nice* they spent more time together than she wanted while he kept talking and could not stop himself. It is important to be assertive, not aggressive nor passive. This is really being *nice* to both of you. If you find yourself having difficulty being assertive, then this is a skill you need to develop to have healthier relationships. There are excellent books, online resources, and counseling that can teach you these skills.

Your home reveals a lot about you. Be sure that you are ready to open this part of you to someone else.

Going to his or her house too soon

One woman reported that she met a man online who sounded most interesting. He was a heart surgeon and they e-mailed several times, talked on the phone, and then met for a lovely romantic dinner. Afterwards he invited her back to his place to see his art collection (etchings?). She accepted, being cultured and all. He indeed did have some nice art, but the best was yet to come. He showed her around his home and when he opened the door to his bedroom, there were shackles and handcuffs attached to the walls and other items of this sort about. The poor dear was absolutely shocked.

This story is one of the most extreme that I heard about and not one that happens that often. But it is good to keep it in mind and remember the Boy Scout motto: "Be prepared!" You just never know.

Telling too much about you too soon

Whoa, hold on there! Telling too much about yourself too soon and at once is not a good thing to do no matter how much you click. So you have met someone and you click and you feel that you can tell him or her deep things about yourself in the early stages of getting to know each other. Of course you want to be open and not just chat about the weather, but reveal yourself slowly, especially the deeper layers and of course previous loves, exes, etc. This also needs to be reciprocal. As you reveal another layer of yourself, he or she should do the same. Do not reveal more about yourself until the other person does some of the same. If these are things about you that only your best friends know, wait until the two of you are very close to best friends. I can tell you from our experiences and those of many others that telling too much too soon backfires. Once you say it, you cannot take it back.

Expectations-great and not so great

Oh boy does this one set us up for a big fall. We read a profile and zingo all our bells ring. This person sounds like everything that we have been searching for. We cannot believe our good fortune. Our blood races and we experience a rush. We cannot wait to contact them to let them know that they are the one for us and we are the one for them. It is important to be optimistic, but building great expectations like these can be very problematic for a variety of reasons. The first is that persons are not always as they seem. People post their most positive attributes, some misrepresent themselves, some are no longer the person they profess to be, and above all no one is perfect. We may also have our blinders on and still believe that there is a prince or princess out there who will ride off into a glorious sunset with us. Tsk tsk tsk, it is time to curb those fantasies because all they will lead to is disappointment, discouragement, and keep you from reaching your goal. **Avoid projecting your fantasies onto the other person.** You create a lot of pressure on yourself and the other person if you consider this one as your likely soul mate. Many persons give up Internet dating because of unrealistic premature expectations. Always proceed slowly and with caution. Be positive and upbeat, but do not count on everything working out. Enjoy the adventure with eyes wide open.

The opposite of this may happen, too and you may expect the worst and this may give you some pleasant surprises, but is more likely to set you up for a negative experience.

Related to great expectations is the fact that Internet dating can be addictive. You may find yourself racing home from work to see your new matches, who emailed you, and who is there for you to email. You find that you are never far from the computer so that you can check your dating site.

You stop to just check in and suddenly find that two hours have passed. You close the door to your office and post the *In Conference* sign on your door. Your great expectations may be getting the best of you and turning you into an online dating junkie. The problem with this is that you probably will spent a lot of time on line, get discouraged, turn off, and then fall offline in disappointment and stay away. What a bumpy ride! Sometimes, too, it is necessary to take a break for a while.

Personalizing rejection

They had their first date and things went very well. They had their second date and he came back to her house. They were having a lovely time. They exchanged kisses and suddenly he got up and said he had to leave and was instantly out the door.

She wondered about her breath or whether there was something wrong with the way she kissed? What did I do? What did I say? Two days passed and he still did not call. She continued to obsess and expand upon what about her turned him off. These are all examples of personalizing something that happened. We feed into our core negative beliefs about ourselves and fill ourselves with reasons that justify that in some way we are not adequate or that something is wrong with us. Fortunately this man was courteous enough to email her and explain his behavior.

I thought it might have passed since it has been a while, but I have a serious allergy to cats. I sneezed for two days after leaving your house. It would be a big problem

for me. Cats are a very big problem.   Sorry. Best of
luck to you.

He did care about her enough to let her know why he was no longer pursuing the relationship. It was not she. In fact it was not her cat, either. It was about him. He was very allergic to cats.

Do not let your fear of rejection keep you from continuing to pursue your goal. Do not let it get you down. Give yourself a go at it again online. **Rejection is not personal.** Some of the most common reasons men and women have given me for rejecting someone as a potential match are 1) there is no initial chemical reaction to your photograph, 2) your profile contains a *deal-breaker*, 3) you contacted someone who has received a deluge of contacts and cannot deal with all of them, 4) you wrote to someone who is playing, 5) you contacted someone who is afraid of relationships, especially committed ones, and 6) the person is intimidated by your photo and/or profile.

Ah, chemistry, chemistry, chemistry. Most of us are looking for that special zing that comes with a chemical reaction to someone, especially if we are looking for an intimate lasting relationship. The chemistry has to be there. Some people think it will come in time, but if your photograph does not light a small spark, chances are that you will be passed over. It is quite likely that you will also react the same way to those who do not appear to come even close to lighting your fire. Chemistry may also fizzle later by the sound of your voice, your first kiss and so forth. This should not send you to voice or kissy school. Chemistry is a very elusive and unpredictable thing. Think about times you have not had a chemical reaction to someone. How did this affect your relationship with him or her? These are people with whom we say we would like to be friends.

We all have our deal-breakers that lead us to reject people as potential matches, just as they have theirs and lead them to reject us. These often involve such things as religious preference, smoking and drinking, height, age, interest in having children, hobbies, attitude towards life, hobbies and interests, and so forth. This type of rejection is not a bad thing. You are who you are and there is someone right for you. Some men may reject a woman who is taller, is not a Victoria Secrets model, or is a vegetarian. This is not a match and it is not personal. Women may reject someone who is shorter than they are, ten years older, not athletic and so forth. To decrease the likelihood of this happening, read the person's profile carefully and see if you do not fit a criterion of importance to him or her. If someone does not appreciate your profile or get hot and steamy over you, they simply are not the one for you. Give people permission to feel this way. Not everyone will drop at your feet no matter who you are. I know a few people (well, very few) who think that Angelina Jolie is not pretty or sexy.

A word of caution here, if most of your contacts are rejecting you, check your photos and your profile out again. Have a friend of the opposite sex examine it and give you feedback. Your photograph may have something in it that is a turnoff—perhaps confusion over whom the person you are with in the photo is—your child or ex? Perhaps you look stern and unapproachable. Your profile may have something in it that turns people off. Do you sound too particular? Too over the top, do you scare people by your accomplishments? Do you sound insincere? Are you carrying around a lot of anger or sadness and excess baggage? Do you present a lot of hurdles for someone to jump over?

Some people, especially those new to the website, receive a deluge of emails and other forms of contacts. This can be overwhelming and take some time to sort out. Online dating is a numbers game and we often eliminate people based on superficial things just to manage. We also make snap judgments about people for reasons we are not clear about.

Some persons, who thankfully are in the minority, are just playing online. I have met several men who seemed mainly to be looking for pen pals or who liked to cyberflirt and cyberdate. These men usually lived a distance away and we exchanged absolutely delightful emails, phone conversations, and photographs. However, when I pressed one of them to meet me in person, he always had an excuse. After a while I caught on to what he really was looking for from me and turned my energies back to meeting someone who was not playing. I was not looking for a pen pal or for someone to entertain through cyberspace. These men are not out to hurt anyone: they just enjoy the game. Some men and women are married and are just out to play in cyberspace, some may be looking for the one-night stand, and others may too afraid to meet a real person and prefer to stay out there in cyberspace. Others may be hiding who knows what. Some people also make up fictitious profiles and there is no real person there. These may be people who want to check out a site that requires one to post a profile. So they make one up and usually do not join the membership and pay the fees. Several men and women have reported that they did this. They were not even members and you were contacting somebody who never existed and is not there to receive your message. There is usually no return to sender to let you know this.

Who, me intimidate someone? I do not think so; I am just a little country boy new to the big city. You may not think that you are scary or threatening to people, but they might see things differently as a result of past experiences, their insecurities and view of whether they consider you out of their league due to education, looks, income etc. and therefore pass you by and you will most likely never know why. So quit the head-trips, psyche searching, and move on. Get back on the Internet and keep searching. If you keep seeing the same faces over and over you may wish to widen your geographical area or switch to another dating site for a while. There are so many to choose from.

You make life painful and defeating for yourself when you give rejection a story and take it personally. You let it feed into core beliefs such as "There is something wrong with me," "I am really unlovable," "No one will love me for who I am". Some people avoid rejection altogether by never taking a risk and never trying. The problem with this is that you live in a safe little lonely protective bubble. You never give yourself the chance to succeed or to fail. So you stay stuck in your storied safe and lonely place. You never challenge these false beliefs and assumptions and allow yourself to find evidence to the contrary. You may also be very good at searching for confirming evidence and unwittingly act in such a way to support those beliefs. This is something that you can work on and need to work on if you want to find companionship.

You have too much baggage

Men or women who are still mourning the loss of a husband, wife, child, parent, sibling, or former flame have too much baggage for anyone but a grief counselor. We have met and viewed people on the Internet who many years after the loss of a spouse still mention their grief in their profile. They unconvincingly state that they are ready for a relationship. Persons who are givers, healers, or controllers might find this appealing, but too much baggage weighs the relationship down and does not allow for much new ground. Do what you need to do to lighten your load. This may involve counseling or therapy. This may be necessary first to release and resolve those things that you are still carrying around with you that prevent you from having healthy relationships with others.

He/She's perfect except for...

They would be perfect if only they would change that one thing. They are everything that I am looking for except for

CRUISING AND BRUISING IN CYBERSPACE

that one thing. This type of thinking often leads to "and I am the one who can heal them. If they love me enough they will change. It's only one thing and I am the one to help them." If this one thing is a minor annoying habit you might have some luck **if it is something they wish to change and is as simple as** folding the newspaper a different way. **Do not go enter into a relationship where that person needs to change in order for the relationship to work.**

Failing to recognize his or her real agenda

Some people lay this out very clearly in their profiles for us while others hide behind platitudes and trite things that everyone says. Here are some examples for you to see if you can pick out what the person's real agenda is from these statements in their profile:

> I am most comfortable on or near the water and have sailed the waters of the U.S. eastern seaboard, Europe, the Bahamas, and the islands of the Caribbean. I live on the water. Are you the person to share a romantic, idyllic future living the marina life and enjoying the sea/ land interface?

Several men reported that some of the women that they contacted made their agenda very clear at the start, usually during their first phone conversation, when they directly asked them such things as: "Will you send my two children to college?"

One woman described an experience with a man whose photograph pictured him as an attractive vigorous looking man. He said that he was honest, open and caring and that he wanted the same thing from a woman. They e-mailed back and forth several times, talked on the phone and then met for lunch. This is how she described the lunch date:

> I did not recognize him and walked past him and he called out my name. I saw some resemblance to the photograph, but this man was much older looking and lacked the vigor he portrayed in this photograph. After exchanging a few niceties and ordering lunch, he got to his agenda. He said that he noticed in my profile that I was in the medical field and wanted my opinion about whether he should have heart surgery or not. He had already gathered opinions from 3 cardiologists and who knows how many others and was still collecting. I am not even a doctor and certainly unable to give an opinion based on how he ate his lunch and what he reported. Plus, when I consult, I certainly charge more than this $10 lunch! All he wanted was a medical opinion and I never heard from him again, thank goodness!

Here is another example of why it is important not to have great expectations and to learn his or her agenda as fast as you can. Luckily this fellow was not into wasting his time either and after his initial hook with his worldly and sophisticated profile and handsome picture, the real deal was clearly spelled out as follows in his second email to her:

> I am looking for a partner for business and for life in the new venture that I am creating internationally. My romantic partner will also be my business partner and invest equally in this with me.

As I mentioned earlier, some people just want to play,

some just want to date a lot, some are looking for sex, some for someone to loan or give them money, some to do business with and so forth. The sooner you get to the real agenda, the better able you will be to determine if this matches your agenda.

They're not that in to you

It is hard for us to deal with this, especially if we are in to him or her and we are taking this personally. I met someone that sounded exactly like the man I wanted to meet. We had so much in common, especially those things which were important to each of us. I felt a surge of excitement and anticipation. Could this be my soul mate? I e-mailed him about how much we had in common and that I was interested in getting to know him better. I received a reply in which he stated that he "had just met someone and wanted to see where that relationship was going. It was too early for me to tell but I want to give it a chance. Would you bear with me for a week and I will email you back?" Two weeks passed and no response. From this it appears 1) he does not keep his word, 2) he is buying time, and 3) that this relationship is working out. I checked him out again several times online and saw that he had been online almost everyday. Hmmmm, this is inconsistent behavior for a guy who is in a relationship and who does not want to meet other women while he is exploring whether that relationship works out. Well, it is time then to recognize that he was just not that in to me. We can tell ourselves all kind of stories and make up all kinds of excuses, but this like it or not, the bottom line is "he's just not into me".

If they do not return your calls, show up when they say they will, do not want to meet your friends, they do not introduce you to their friends, or come to events you plan, chances are good that they are not that in to you. You want to learn to pick up on this as soon as you can so that you do not waste your time. Do you want to spend your time waiting around for someone who is not there in the first place? What keeps us from identifying this is our unwillingness to see the situation as it really is. Telling you they were too busy to call, they just want to be friends, or just not following through are big signs not to miss. Here is another example:

> They met for their first date and had a great time. The chemistry was there as he demonstrated by his passionate attempts later that night to get her into bed. She enjoyed the kissing, but she stopped at that. He said he would call her the next day. Three days later he called and asked her out for two nights later. They set the time for 7pm. She was dressed and awaiting her Don Juan. The minutes ticked on, then the hours. At 9:00 she admitted to herself he was not going to be there. She hoped that nothing bad had happened to him and made excuses with accident fantasies. He called her the next day and chatted as if nothing happened. She asked him what happened to him last night. He told her, "Oh, I got home late from work, had dinner, and then watched some TV." She mentioned that they had plans for last night. He was genuinely confused, "We did?". He did not even remember that he had made a date with her.

The example above really covers two areas: 1) He's not that in to you and 2) It's all about me. Even he recognized that there was no excuse he could give.   Here is another experience:

> They had their first date and laughed and looked into each other's eyes a lot. When she kissed him goodnight she felt great chemistry and thought he did too. She even swooned for a few minutes after the kiss. He said he would call her tomorrow. Tomorrow, tomorrow, tomorrow... Three tomorrows later she e-mailed him and thanked him for the wonderful dinner and time. He e-mailed her back and said that he had a great time too and that he was leaving town in 5 days because his mother was very ill and he would call when he got back. She e-mailed him back and said that she hoped everything would be all right with his mother and that if he just wanted someone to talk to, please call. He e-mailed back, thank you and that his mother was dying and a few other nice words because he was a nice southern boy. During the next week and a half she noticed that he was checking into the online dating site every day.

Hmmmm, he is too busy to call her, but not too busy to check out the online action?? There were not many excuses that she could make up for him. She got the point.

Then there was the spy who left her cold:

> My profession requires that I travel from time to time. My dog and I do counter and anti-terror work so we never know when we are needed. We may be traveling for a week or so. This is one thing that I cannot control right now due to world issues.

He never contacted her again. Do these guys really admit they do this and if so, why are they on an online dating site?

Ouch, yes this can hurt and disappointments happen. However, if you make the mistake of taking it personally, you really set yourself up for all kinds of negative stories and beliefs about yourself. Do not let this minor disappointment beat you up. Go back and re-read the section on not taking things personally if you do, because **not taking this personally** is something that is very important for you to work on. Someone may not be our cup of tea and there is nothing wrong with him or her, just as we may not strike someone's fancy and there is nothing wrong with us. Scientists and all sorts of others have been trying for ages to figure out what this thing is that attracts persons to each other besides just chemistry. So far no one has come up with the answer. It is the million-dollar question.

Let me call you sweetheart

These persons may do your ego good, but you also feel a little creepy about how quickly you become their "darling" and "sweetheart". They are quick to put you on intimate and endearing terms often within an e-mail or two. They are quick to latch on to you and form a relationship. This behavior scared several of my respondents away, so I am unable to say what would have happened if they pursued the relationship. It was too much, too soon to be real.

SET YOUR RADAR FOR THESE

Common and uncommon liars

One of the biggest complaints I have heard about online dating is the amount of lies people tell about themselves. It is almost commonly expected that those over 40 lie about their age and seem to have found the fountain of youth. Married persons pose as single, and others claim to be thin and suddenly when you meet them they are markedly fluffier than they described. Some people have reported that a person used a photograph of someone else. Unfortunately it may appear that everyone who dates online is hiding or misrepresenting something. They may have low self-esteem and not be happy with aspects of themselves. However, do not automatically pardon their lie because they may lack self-esteem. Liars are afraid to tell the truth about some aspect of themselves or behavior because the truth will not get them what they want. I must admit here, though, that I have lied about my age. When I turned the big 60, I magically seemed to enter a new dating category. One day I was 59 and hearing from people my own age and the next day I was 60 and generally hearing from a much more senior crowd. So I shaved 2 years off my age, yet retained very current photographs. In my essay I did state my true age. It is sad that ageism rages in such ways.

Unfortunately lying is rarely an isolated incident and if he or she lied once, it is likely it will happen again and again and yes, again and so forth; especially if he or she does not admit it right up front without being asked. These are people who know the truth will not get them what they want. I have also met people on line who were direct and honest in their profiles and immediately stated that they were not divorced for certain reasons, had herpes, and so forth. I have a tremendous respect for these men and women who have the courage to tell the truth about themselves in spite of its consequences. Speaking of truth and consequences, lies do have their consequences. How long can the liar keep up the façade? Lies may buy you time, but time eventually runs out. There is no undergarment that can pull in 40 pounds (and where would the pounds go?); plastic surgery for every part of your body, botox for all sags and bags, and wives are hard to hide and rarely stay put. If you say you are a surgeon and really a longshoreman, your hands may give you away! If you say that you are 6'0" and are really 5'7" your date is definitely going to notice. Until you are comfortable with yourself as you are, you cannot expect to find true love. Liars hurt themselves more than anyone else because this pretty much ends the relationship now or later down the road.

The following subsections discuss more common to less common lies. My goal in writing this is not to discourage you from online dating, but to make you smarter and better able to recognize these and not waste your time being duped. We all have been taken in, even in traditional dating, but our goal is to be cybersmart and not make the same mistake twice. Be cautious and keep on the alert. There is no need for you to be paranoid and think everyone is lying, because not everyone is. Expect honesty, but do not be surprised to find the opposite. How and when you find out is very important. Do your part and tell the truth. So set your radar for the following lies.

Age and weight

Age and weight are the most common lies. In fact, many men and women reported experiences with persons being grossly untruthful about these. I hardly recognized one man I had a lunch date with because he was at least 15 years older than his picture. Many persons, especially men, reported that they have come to expect lies about age in particular, especially among those over forty years of age. To compensate for this, many lie about their age and/or set their preferred age range for a partner lower than they normally would. Of course, this then continues the cycle of false age. One clever man that I had a date with, had already checked my age out on a website that somehow has access to people's ages and thank goodness I was really 59 at the time.

To detect how old the photograph might be, pay attention to the hairstyle, clothing, and anything else that might date it. Note differences among posted photographs. I also check out the accuracy of the person's age during the phone conversation phase by simply casually asking the person, "Is your age really __?" Sometimes photographs can give you an indication of weight by what is shown as well as not shown. For example a person who only has photos of their head and face may be keeping more under the table than you are led to think. Listen and look carefully. Ask questions. This may sound rude, but you are really screening each other for potential dates and these issues can become deal breakers. **Be assertive, not aggressive, and ask about things that are important to you.**

Health status

Health status is another subject some are reluctant to reveal. This is a *catch-22*. If you reveal a problem right up front, it might limit you meeting someone. However, revealing it later might also have the same result and you have invested more. If you are in really good health and shape, this is something that you would definitely want to state in your profile.

Watch for indicators of health problems. As people get older, they are more and more likely to have them. I have met several men with the telltale scars in the middle of their chests that indicate open-heart surgery. Again, do not be afraid to ask about health status. This should not be your opening line, but slip it in there somewhere.

Marital status

The state of the union is another area that some parties lie about. The following profile did not have a photograph.

His profile read, "Refined, (even distinguished) handsome, intelligent, and witty are adjectives used to describe me." He said that he was a retired lawyer and that he was 62 years old. He grew up in a "caring, privileged, loving family. He said that he was looking for a "very attractive, refined, intelligent, upscale and interesting woman who appreciates what life has to offer including the finer "things in life'.". He did not post a photo. He also stated that his ideal relationship was "caring about someone even more than you care about yourself...sharing in the wonders of life and understanding and attending to the needs of each other."

Red Flag 1: Remember what I said earlier about no photos? It does not usually mean that they are so high profile that they do not wish to post their mug shot. It often means that they do not want to be seen for a specific reason. Online dating is so common now and so many people do it, that there is no shame in being seen online looking for a date, unless of course you are in a committed relationship and sneaking about outside of it. He or she also may not post a photograph for the common reasons stated above such as age, weight etc. Sometimes they tell you, "Oh, I don't have a recent photo." Duh, if you are making the effort to write a profile and try to meet someone, then get photos taken. You can buy disposable digital cameras now and presto you are ready to load your picture up to the site.

Hopefully several red flags were raised for you with this profile.

Red Flag 2: Would a refined and distinguished man describe himself this way with all his stellar qualities? I ran this by a few refined and distinguished men that I knew and they said, "absolutely not". I looked at profiles of some men that I had met who were classy guys and they did not describe themselves in this manner. So we have a very suspicious profile here.

> When she read this profile her red flags waved and her BS detector rang loudly enough to set off all the car alarms within a 5-mile radius. She decided to see what this character was up to. She sent him a pleasant short initial e-mail. He sent her an inviting one back. She e-mailed him again and asked him if he was married. He responded that he was divorced. He gave her his cell phone number and asked her to call him.
>
> She called; they talked and in the course of things he mentioned that he was currently separated. She quickly picked up on the inconsistencies in his story and said, "I thought you were divorced." He explained he had been separated for the past 3 months and the divorce had been filed.
>
> She was one smart cookie who knew the ins and outs of her online dating service. Well, this particular one included when the person began on line. She noted that he had been online for over a year. She confronted him with this and he quickly babbled on about how they had been divorced, got back together, separated got remarried and all sorts of BS. Now the car alarms were going off for a 100-mile radius. He finally gave up and said in awe, "Wow, you are really smart to have figured that out! Yes, I am really married. Wow, I should have known you'd be so smart." She told him that he was a cad and that the nicest thing he could do for his wife was to give her an easy and quick divorce.

Here is another one for you with a nice photo of a good-looking man:

Divorced man. I am not proud that I am divorced, but it is better than being in a relationship that can no longer work. I am very straightforward. She emailed him that he sounded very interesting. He emailed her back. They emailed back and forth several times. Then he gave her his number and asked her to call. They talked for a while and then he told her that he had something he needed to tell her. He was married and would not be divorced for three more years. His wife would not grant the divorce until she was eligible for his Social Security, which was three more years. They were no longer involved with each other and each openly dated.

And here's another one for you:

He said that he was divorced. They emailed, they talked on the phone (he gave her only his cell phone number), and they started a delightful relationship. They went out to dinner; he spent the weekends with her at her house. They were having a grand romance. She began to wonder after several months why he never invited her to his house. Eventually she asked him. He told her, "I live with my ex-wife until the house is sold. She lives in the other half of the house. We are on very bad terms with each other, but I cannot move out before the house is sold, because I am afraid that she will take my things that I must leave in the house so the house will sell."

She was not happy about this to say the least, but his disdain for his ex-wife was convincing. She thought the arrangement was crazy and not the healthiest. Yet she figured it was his business and no threat to their relationship, just an inconvenience and she liked to be at her house anyway. Several months later she asked him point blank, "Are you divorced?" He changed the subject. She changed it back and confronted him with the question again. He wiggled and tried to avoid answering it again. She continued with her direct questioning. He finally admitted, "No, but it will be settled in the next month. We have a court date and are working out the settlement."

Yee gads, once a liar, always a liar? She should have learned the first time that he would lie about things that might jeopardize their relationship and not be to his benefit. In fact, he had already lied to her once about his health status, but told her only when he needed surgery. It took her almost 5 months to get the truth about his real marital status and living situation. The man in the previous scenario at least told the truth about his marital status early in the relationship before they actually met. He also told her voluntarily on his own. So take heed, be sure to ask direct questions and it is a red flag if: **Red Flag 1:** they do not invite you to their home and Red **Flag 2:** they have a difficult time answering you when you ask how long they have been divorced. Some clever ones hedge here and tell you how long they have been divorced from their first wife, but neglect to answer your question in relation to their second wife. Ask direct specific questions and look for omissions and inconsistencies. You have the right to know and to ask.

What do you think about this one?

Multimillionaire teacher/businessman, 6 ft. 176 lbs. No hang-ups, above average looking, no debts, Mercedes, house $400,000 range. (No photo)

If you said, it's a crock; you are most likely right on. This person is doing a put on for whatever reasons. Hopefully his put-on put you off.

It's all about me

We have all met our share of narcissists. However, when you are in such a relationship you soon come to realize that there is only room for that person and that your role is to play the mirror and reflect back to him or her how wonderful he or she is. No criticism is tolerated. There is little room and regard for your feelings and needs because for them the relationship is "all about me." They are self-absorbed and often needy. If you should happen to come to this person for support and comfort, you will be disappointed. There is very little tolerance, interest, and support there for you. The **conversation will quickly turn back to him or her. Watch out carefully for this Red Flag.** Here are some examples:

> He wrote a very witty and long treatise about himself for his profile. She decided to contact him. He emailed her a 3 page single spaced witty biography about himself. She was impressed-- no one, especially a man wrote so much and shared so much about himself before. "How special," she thought. She decided to reciprocate and e-mail him a witty biography about herself. She spent two days working on it. She sent it. He invited her to call him. She called him on his cell phone and they briefly talked. He said that his son and daughter-in-law lived in her city. They were doing their residencies. She asked what field his daughter-in-law was in. He said he did not know and his tone of voice indicated

that he did not care. She did not hear from him again until several months later when she received an e-mail from him stating that he saw her profile online and was interested in learning more about her. He sent her his long biography. Yes, the same one he had sent her several months ago. She replied: "Oh, how quickly they forget. You contacted me several months ago and it seems you do not even remember."

What can we say about this guy except, "it's all about him"? His daughter in law is a medical resident and he does not even care what field she is in?

The real agenda

He describes himself in his profile as a lawyer; his photo shows a fairly attractive smiling man dressed in a suit and tie. His profile is well written. He says that he is athletic, romantic, emotionally secure, HONEST, and loves to give presents and that family is important to him. She e-mails him and he tells her "Your letter was the best I have ever received." He continues to charm her. They speak on the phone. Next they set a date to meet in a public bar/restaurant for a drink Saturday night. He is an hour late. Unfortunately, she waited. He tells her he fell asleep. She was not impressed.

After their drink, he asks her to go for a walk on the beach next to this restaurant and again, unfortunately, she agrees. He begins his play, she blocks his pass, he tackles her, she calls foul and turns back to the restaurant. This continues several times before they are off this playing field.

They go out on a few more dates. He is cheap, but

verbally plays the big shot. She is ready to break it off with him during their next date. He arrives and is a new person—he is attentive, interested in her needs, and wants to do the things that she likes to do. They spend the weekend together. Monday morning he awakes with her and appears despondent and sits with his head in his hands. She asks him, 'What's wrong?" He tells her that he has this big business investment and needs $10,000 that day or he will lose all that he has put into it. She gives him coffee and sympathy. He then pops the question, "Will you lend me $10,000?" She may have made some mistakes with this guy, but this was one she was smart enough to avoid. She tried to help him problem solve his options. He kept giving her options where she could get him the $10,000. He then left and said he had to talk to the other party and see if he could arrange something. If not, he said that he was in deep trouble. She was worried he would do something drastic. She asked him to call her back later that day, that she was concerned about him. He calls her back the next day and says, "I have good news and I have bad news." She takes the bait, "Tell me." He says that the other party will accept $5000 but it has to be now." He proceeds to tell her that she can get cash from her credit card, she could ask her parents, etc. She firmly replies, "No." End of story. She does not hear from him again.

It is not too hard to figure out the real agenda here. I do not want you to think that this is unique to online dating. You meet all types of people and the sooner you can get to the real agenda with anyone you meet to date, the better. In this example, there were a few very subtle clues early on. However, red flags warnings should wave with a drastic change in behavior. **Do not loan someone you are dating money.** People who have done so often appear on TV shows such as Dr. Phil and Judge Alex.

Then we have the people who are coming to town and looking for a date while they are visiting family and need a diversion, on vacation, and so forth. They want someone in each port of call. This is their agenda. So note in your online dating site where this person actually lives. The best you can hope for here is a short time of fun and then possibly a long-distance relationship. At least you know the score.

> I'm looking for a very down to earth, bubbly, non-confrontational, easy-going, adventurous soul mate to spend the rest of my life with, who shares common interests, quality values and family. Total trust and a monogamous relationship is critical.

Ah, thankfully there are many men and women who are really looking for a great and lasting monogamous relationship. However, what does he or she mean by "non-confrontational"? This could mean non-argumentative, not aggressive, not assertive and in fact a "yes" person.

Control freaks

See if you can pick up on some of the clues from these excerpts from his profile:

> Please read what I am looking for before you respond. I am a very caring, sensitive, and easily hurt person who lives life to the fullest. I don't do fine dining until we take the relationship to the next level. An evening

CRUISING AND BRUISING IN CYBERSPACE

of fine dining without romance isn't fine dining. I like to meet first for a drink. Then, I have restaurants on my get acquainted list and those of my approved list including my private clubs, etc., etc. If we go to phase 2 of getting to know each other, then I like to eat at one of my clubs as opposed to public restaurants.

Is there anything more I need to say about this? Well, I will. The lady went out with him and it seems he had many many rules and should have given her a print out so she knew what they all were. He became quite sullen and angry when she violated one of his rules she did not know about (she was supposed to kiss him during dinner and hold his hand). She did thank him for a lovely evening and lightly kissed him goodnight, but this did not make up for the during dinner rule.

Freaked about controllers

This man or woman is so freaked out about being controlled that he or she sees control issues everywhere. When you say, "Hi, nice day isn't it?" he or she will immediately think, "Now you are telling me how I am to feel about this day. You cannot control me like that!" OK, so I gave another extreme example here. This one, I actually made up. But persons who are freaked out about being controlled will give you many clues because they are hypersensitive to anything they perceive as an act to control them. Simple requests can be seen as control issues. It is very hard to relate with someone who is so on the defensive because so much of his or her energy is spent this way. They have a difficult time trusting and loving. Relationships are ambivalent at best.

Should you want more information on dating, consult the Internet, your local bookstores, friends, and so forth for more information. Just remember, *nothing ventured, nothing gained.* Just go into things with your eyes wide open and pay attention to your gut and curb those expectations and personalizations. They cause so much pain and are self-defeating.

NUMBER 47

Please do not be put off by the some of the characters I have introduced you to in this book. I focused mainly on these to give you some skills in recognizing, learning, and dealing with them. You will find these persons in any type of dating encounter and the sooner you can deal with them, the better. Online dating is a wonderful opportunity to meet a wide variety of available persons who are looking for a relationship. The age of the computer is upon us and provides wonderful opportunities to search for our match.

This section describes only a few of the very many success stories of online dating. Numerous persons reported meeting very wonderful people online with whom they had delightful relationships. For various reasons some of these relationships ran their course and ended, others became friendships, and some relationships continue to grow and thrive and result in long-term affairs, partnerships, or marriage.

I called this section Number 47 in honor of a couple that met online.

> He had been online for some time and dated 46 women with whom he did not click. She was the 47th one and they dated and had so much fun together. Eventually she moved in with him and the fun, joy, and love deepened. They shared many things and now are happily married.

I have heard of many stories like these and they make the cruising and bruising all worthwhile. It takes time, effort, and perseverance, lightening your baggage and learning from your mistakes. Give yourself time to figure it out and be resilient.

No matter what the outcome of each online adventure, people reported learning more about themselves and others through their online dating experiences. Each experience teaches you more about yourself, introduces you to different ways of thinking, and generally helps you learn more about what you need to resolve in order to find what you are looking for. For example, when I began online dating, I learned that I had not yet resolved my feelings about my deceased husband. I needed to complete this before I could relate healthfully with someone else. I had to do this first. Then I would be better able to search for the type of man I thought I was looking for.

I met many wonderful men, some bruisers, and several men who also had excess baggage of their own. Each of these experiences has taught me invaluable lessons. I have joyfully come back in touch with parts of myself that I have not experienced in many years. I learned more about what I could not accept—the so-called *"deal-breakers"* and the *"must haves"*. I met many different people whom I would never otherwise have met and each one taught me something valuable. For example, I learned that I did not want to be in a relationship with someone who would not recognize and express his feelings or share and be open. From another man, I was encouraged to deepen my spirituality, and from another, I learned more about music. I learned to recognize more quickly the self-centered fellows and the genuinely warm and sincere ones. I learned about a singles sailing club, which I subsequently joined and made many new male and female friends and established sailing connections. I also had a good time getting to know a variety of people through online dating.

I end this book by urging you to start with and maintain a positive attitude and outlook. It is highly unlikely that you will find the right one and fall in love in a month. As you cruise, yes, you will bruise some. You did when you learned to walk, too, and look at you now. It is inevitable that to find your special someone you will encounter many persons who are not. You will reject others and they will reject you. If your self-esteem is in poor condition this can be a rough highway for you. Honesty and self-confidence are important qualities to have for any type of dating relationship.

People are interesting and, let me repeat, they can teach us so much. Each brings a gift into our lives, although it may take us some time to realize what that gift is. Keep your perspective! We learn by our successes and our failures. Becoming your authentic you is an ongoing process and through trial and error, or cruising and bruising in cyberspace, you will move further along the path of finding the right match for you.

"Good night and good luck." (I stole that quote from Edward R. Murrow. If you do not know who he is, you can learn all about him on the Internet.)